STORMS OF PERFECTION

VOLUME III

STORMS OF PERFECTION

VOLUME III

ANDY ANDREWS

Distributed by:
INTERNET SERVICES CORPORATION
USA
BK442

Books are available at quantity discounts to schools, civic organizations, corporations, and small businesses. For information please write to: Marketing Division, Lightning Crown Publishers, P.O. Box 17321, Nashville, TN 37217.

Published in Nashville, Tennessee by Lightning Crown Publishers P.O. Box 17321, Nashville, TN 37217.

The Bible verses used in this publication are from the New American Standard Version and the New King James Version. Used by permission.

Printed in the United States of America.

FIRST EDITION
First Printing: May 1996

Library of Congress Catalog Card Number: 95-081473
ISBN 0-9620620-5-8

Editor: Robert D. Smith
Front Cover Photo: Corel Professional Photos
Back Cover Photo: Dennis Carney
Book Design: Payne Art Design
Cover Design: Publishers Design Service

LIGHTNING
CROWN
PUBLISHERS

P.O. Box 17321 • Nashville, TN 37217
1-800-726-2639

What They're Saying. . .

*"James Allen wrote, 'Dream lofty dreams and as you dream, so shall you become!' **Storms of Perfection** embodies that sentiment to perfection!"*
Pete Babcock
VICE PRESIDENT & GENERAL MANAGER OF THE ATLANTA HAWKS

*"The ideas and principles of **Storms of Perfection** are inspiring, especially because they are expressed in the words of the people who live them."*
Tom Monaghan
FOUNDER OF DOMINO'S PIZZA, INC.

"Very inspirational stories for those trying to succeed in any field or life in general."
Coach Joe Paterno
HEAD FOOTBALL COACH – PENN STATE UNIVERSITY

"Inspiring stories to help every reader rise above problems. A valuable collection of fifty-two achievements perfect for every bookshelf."
Robin Leach
HOST, LIFESTYLES OF THE RICH AND FAMOUS

*"**Storms of Perfection** is a wonderful idea that should have been done many years ago. I love reading about the success of others, and this book will be an inspiration to many. "*
Crystal Gayle
ENTERTAINER

*"**Storms of Perfection** is a book filled with hope for everyone striving to achieve the American dream."*
Jack Kemp
CO-DIRECTOR OF EMPOWER AMERICA
FORMER SECRETARY OF HOUSING AND URBAN DEVELOPMENT

*"**Storms of Perfection** will let young people know that it's okay to experience setbacks, failures and hardships. It's a natural part of the process of success."*
Lou Holtz
HEAD FOOTBALL COACH
UNIVERSITY OF NOTRE DAME

"Full of examples of great achievements despite personal and professional adversity and setbacks."
Joan Rivers
COMEDIENNE/AUTHOR/TALK SHOW HOST

TABLE OF CONTENTS

ACKNOWLEDGEMENTS

Thank you to my wife, Polly, and my manager, Robert D. Smith, who both played an important and critical part in the areas of encouragement, instruction, and inspiration.

Special thanks to Shane Ray, Isabel Galindo, Alejandra Galindo, Sandie Dorff, Max Reed, Brian Williams, and Chad Poindexter for their creative input in all phases of this production.

Special acknowledgement to Martha Luker Hales for her expertise and brilliant editing.

My sincere appreciation goes to Barbara Hill, Susan Swann, Norma Paz, Cheryl Loverde, Lance Carter, Barbara Drucker, Joe Lake, Vaughan M. Doty, Maggie Raimo, Steven Thomas, Carla Ferrigno, Heidi Bookout, Ronald Miller, Neil Stalter, Chaz Corzine, Hal Wetherman, Norma Paten, Rick Delsasso, Fred Westbrook, and John Parker for their invaluable assistance, advice, and help with the letter participants.

Grateful acknowledgement is expressed to Lucy Andrews, Joey Alvarez, Michael Harrison, Patrick McCurley, Carson Poindexter, Tim & Connie Foley, Ellis & Doraine Lucas, Bubba & Sandy Pratt, and Dexter & Birdie Yager for their encouragement and belief in this project.

PREFACE

*(EDITOR'S NOTE: This preface is reprinted from **Storms of Perfection I** in order to explain the concept of the title.)*

I was seven years old, barely keeping pace as my father strode purposefully through the woods, the dry brush crackling under our feet. August was rarely pleasant in the deep South, but this year had been especially hot; especially dry.

Walking the densely forested stand of timber that day, young as I was, I was acutely aware of my father's mood. The month-long drought our area was experiencing had him worried. I watched in silence as he broke dry twigs from seemingly lifeless trees and examined the wilting, dull color of the new growth under them. We hiked through the dust of the parched creek bed, following it to the beaver pond where our family often came for picnics. The pond was nearly empty and the beaver lodge, usually a site of frantic activity, stood abandoned on dry land.

Without warning, the wind shifted. With the change in direction came a rapid increase in velocity and a perceptible drop in temperature. It became cool within a matter of seconds, as the wind, whistling above, threatened to send branches crashing down around us. Lightning and thunder worked the atmosphere almost simultaneously, creating explosions of light and sound that terrified me. My father, his arms wrapped around me tightly, was also afraid...and grateful.

He was grateful for this violent performance of nature and the hope of water that came with it. As the trees bent with the wind and the thunder covered my cries, my father sat down, pulled me into his lap and said, "Don't worry. You'll be all right. Something good is going to come out of this. Be still. Be patient."

As he comforted me, the rain came. Not with the gentle drops I had seen in the past, but in wild, silver sheets bursting all around us. It wound through the limbs and leaves, over rocks and deep into the tangled thickets leaving nothing untouched.

And then, as suddenly as it had begun – it was over. The thunder and lightning and wind and rain were gone, their energy exhausted. It was still again, but even at my young age, I noticed a difference. The forest wasn't just still...it was calm.

With his hand, my father wiped the drops of water from my face. Only my deep sobs betrayed the presence of tears, not raindrops, on my cheeks. Then he smiled, wrung out the front of his shirt, and motioned toward the pond. "It'll fill back up now," he said, "and those beavers will be able to spend the winter here like they'd planned."

We turned in time to see a doe and her fawn drinking from the already flowing creek. The frogs had started their own chorus as we headed for home. "Ahh," my father breathed deeply, "everything just smells clean, doesn't it?" And it did. The very air, which only a short time ago had been hot and dirty, now seemed almost sweet. "Let's sit down by this big oak, Son," he said quietly. "I have something to tell you."

I snuggled in beside him, and in very nearly a whisper, he began. "You know," he said, watching me from the corner of his eye, "you weren't the only one scared a little while ago. Those deer were afraid, too. The squirrels huddled together as close as they could get and what with all the crashes and booms, well, I'm pretty sure the rabbits were worried. But now, something important has happened. The very event that frightened everyone in the forest turned out to be exactly what they needed."

"Do you hear the birds?" I nodded. "Remember how quiet they were before the rain? Now they're hopping around, chirping, drinking from puddles, and feasting on the worms that come out only when the ground is wet. The fish in the pond have more oxygen to breathe and cooler water to swim in. The dust that was on all the plants has been washed away so they are much cleaner for the rabbits and deer to eat. Nobody likes dirty food."

"In fact, Son, all of us are better off now than we were an hour ago. Just because of the storm. What looked like the worst – turned out to be the best. It was a storm of perfection."

*　*　*

My dad has been gone for well over a decade, but I can remember that day in the woods as if it happened this morning. Writing this now, I couldn't begin to count the instances I've had reason to recall his words. There have been many storms in my life; and some were more terrifying than that day when when I was seven. I do try, however, to keep my father's lesson in my heart. And it is easy to hear him tell me, "Don't worry. You'll be all right. Something good is going to come out of this. Be still. Be patient. It's only a storm of perfection."

AUTHOR'S NOTE

Welcome to the third collection of letters in the *Storms of Perfection* series. During the past few years I have become more convinced than ever that we are all a product of the storms we endure. Each of us, at this very moment, is either struggling with a storm, exiting a storm or entering one. These sometimes tragic problems are a constant in our lives and they, quite literally, shape our daily existence.

A wise man once said, "Life is 10% what happens to you and 90% how you deal with it." Is that true? Do we, in essence, individually determine the quality and direction of our lives? The answer, I believe, is yes!

As you turn the pages of this book, remember to be encouraged by the storms presented here. Every participant in this collection is a winner - a success. Their victories, however, were not by chance, but by choice. The same is true of your future victories and successes. They depend solely on the decisions and attitude you bring to your storm.

The people included here want you to understand that problems are a molding point for success. What looks like the worst can often turn out to be the best. A *Storm of Perfection* is a challenge allowed in your life to mold you, shape you, fire you, and prepare you for the success in your future. People forget that even in the Bible God did not save Daniel from the lion's den - He saved Daniel *in* the lion's den because He knew it would be good for Daniel.

By the time you find the letter in this book that most closely relates to you, you will have come to the realization that all the participants in the project used a goal or dream as an umbrella during their storms. It is imperative that we all identify a reason to weather the problems in our lives. That is perhaps the additional lesson these people teach - that not only are storms a necessary part of the success process, but that the thing most important to accomplish in your life can be the fuel that brings a storm to its perfection. After all, no person without a dream ever made a dream come true.

Andy Andrews
Gulf Shores, Alabama

Dedication to Melissa Outlaw,
whose courage in facing her storms
has been an inspiration to me.

ZIG ZIGLAR

MOTIVATIONAL SPEAKER/ AUTHOR

...is Chairman of the Zig Ziglar Corporation. He travels the world over, delivering his messages of humor, hope and enthusiasm to audiences of all kinds and sizes.

I am proud to say that Zig is a friend of mine. I jump at every chance I get to hear Zig speak, or to read his books. Zig has literally helped thousands of people achieve success in life by sharing with them his acute understanding of the qualities of success, motivation and setting and reaching goals. Zig's humor, down to earth principles and inspirational wisdom are reminiscent of the late Will Rogers.

Zig Ziglar is truly a wonderful person, who is sincere in his instruction - a man who "walks his talk." It is no surprise that Zig's captivating, enthusiastic personality and eloquent speaking ability has made him one of the most sought-after speakers in the world. And, as one of the nation's most accomplished writers, Zig's work has been translated into seven languages. He has written ten celebrated books on personal growth, leadership, sales, faith, family and success. His latest book, *Over the Top,* was released in May of 1994.

Zig started out as a front line salesman. He developed his expertise in sales until he rose to the top of his field. He turned his career to full time public speaking in 1970 and has been in high demand ever since. I have found a wealth of wisdom in reading the works of Zig Ziglar... here is a small sample.

The Zig Ziglar Corporation

THE TRAINING COMPANY ™

Zig Ziglar
Chairman

Mr. Andy Andrews
Post Office Box 2761
Gulf Shores, Alabama 36547

Dear Andy:

I'm truly one of the most fortunate people who ever lived. Throughout my life, whenever I have had a real need, someone has always been there to help me. To recognize and honor those individuals, I have a "Wall of Gratitude" in my office displaying the pictures of those significant people. However, like everyone else, I have had my disappointments, defeats, frustrations and set-backs. Some have been significant; many of minor consequence. I would like to share the most disappointing, frustrating experience of my life and its impact on me.

A number of years ago while living in Atlanta, Georgia, I was involved in the sale of a sleep-teaching course. It worked quite well in my own personal life and I was enormously excited about the possibilities. As a result, I was really "gung-ho" about selling the program.

I was given the states of Alabama, Georgia and Florida as part of a significantly larger franchise. I immediately set national records and gained considerable recognition. The author of the course was a nationally-known, highly-regarded individual. He and the franchise owner were at odds, which caused me some concern. One day the author came to Atlanta to visit with me. My wife and I had dinner with him, and in the course of conversation I expressed my concern about my future if he and the franchise owner parted company. He assured me that I would be permitted to retain my territory. He said he was even considering appointing me his National Sales Manager. We parted with a warm handshake and friendly, encouraging words.

About three weeks later I received a special delivery letter, telling me that I had just lost the state of Alabama, the office and sales force in Mobile and the office and sales force in Pensacola, Florida. The thing that made this particularly devastating was the fact that we had just survived a six-week strike when we had no merchandise to sell. Since the business was new, we were short on cash before the strike took place. This devastating blow, reducing my territory and eliminating well over 50% of my trained organization, was a bitter pill to swallow.

Since I personally had no specific contract, even for the remaining territory, and since this individual had specifically lied to me once, my trust factor was zero. Truthfully, my spirit was

3330 Earhart, Suite 204 • Carrollton, Texas 75006 • (214) 233-9191 • Fax (214) 991-1853 broken, I was frustrated and discouraged. For nearly a week I literally did almost nothing. But with three children and a wife to support, I had to come out of that despondent mood in order to survive. I took the first opportunity that came along. The training I received bordered on zero and my attitude was still truly bad. I believe I made two or three half-hearted calls with no results.

Fortunately, at that time an opportunity to sell securities to build a paper mill in South Georgia came my way and I was able to regain a sense of perspective and accomplish some worthwhile goals.

When the stock offering was over, I decided to get back into the cook ware business where I had previously spent eight successful years. This experience enabled me to re-establish myself, set some more records and gain a degree of financial stability. In short, I landed on my feet.

As I evaluate my reaction to being mistreated by a "celebrity," I realize I went through some very tough times. I believe in my own heart that had I not been taught from childhood to accept responsibility, it would have been infinitely more difficult for me to start over. It was also a huge plus that I loved my wife and my three little girls and that they trusted and depended on me. The love and responsibility were tremendously important in digging me out of the "dumps."

Was there one incident or one day? How did I pick myself up? I believe it was through necessity and the fact that the word "quit" was not in my vocabulary. On occasion I've had to pause before I went forward, or I've had to reposition myself by advancing in the opposite direction (as I did in this particular case). But deep down I just knew that somehow, some way it was going to work out.

What did I learn and what can I share with your readers, Andy, that will enable them to be more successful in their own lives? The major benefit to me came as a result of a major disappointment in this particular gentleman, combined with a similar disappointment in another celebrity writer/speaker. I promised myself that if I ever "made it" or achieved any degree of success in my chosen profession, I would make every effort to be consistent in my perceived public personality and the personality that my friends, family and associates knew. In short, I wanted to be consistent in both word and deed. Over the years, I believe that has been a major contributing factor in my career as a speaker and writer.

Hope this is of value to you and your readers, Andy.

SEE YOU OVER THE TOP!

Zig Ziglar

ZZ/lm

Important footnote: The two men who disappointed me the most had more specific, positive influence on my life and career than most of the men and women who were marvelous role models and teachers, because many people had shown me what I should do to be successful, but these two showed me what I should not do. Which just proves that it's not what happens to you that determines your future - it's how you choose to perceive and respond to what happens to you that truly determines your future.

DENNIS WALTERS

PROFESSIONAL GOLFER

... is the only person paralyzed below the waist who earns a living as a professional golfer

Dennis Walters received a lot of opinions when his legs were paralyzed in a golf cart accident at the age of 24. None were supportive of his dream to become a professional golfer. Dennis Walters is now the only professional golfer who has no use of his legs.

The "Dennis Walters Golf Show" has been called golf's most inspiring hour. It has been viewed by millions in person and on national television programs such as "That's Incredible," "Good Morning America" and "PM Magazine." Dennis performs at PGA and LPGA tour events, amateur and collegiate golf tournaments, business seminars, corporate meetings, trade shows and golf clubs across the US and Canada.

Dennis simply is a class individual who brings warmth, joy and an inspirational message to people from all walks of life. He enthusiastically delivers a message of determination and the power of a winning attitude. With such a "can-do" philosophy, Dennis Walters overcame incredible odds to return to the game he loves, and the game of golf hasn't been the same since. He beats his handicap every time he plays.

"One hour of golf mastery and human inspiration."

Andy Andrews
PO Box 2761
Gulf Shores, Alabama 36547

Dear Andy,

Since the age of 8, my goal in life was to be a professional golfer. The obstacle that was placed in my path was a formidable one. At the age of 24, I had an accident that left me paralyzed from the waist down. Needless to say, my whole life changed and my dreams seemed to have no chance of coming true.

After the accident, I found that there were a lot of things I could not do, but there was no way that I was going to give up playing golf. Even on my darkest days, my love of the game, helped sustain me. I am also lucky to have a loving and supportive family, who helped me through those very difficult months.

I began my road back to playing golf by hitting balls from a wheelchair and later I advanced to playing from a swivel seat that was mounted on the passenger side of a golf cart. This gave me the freedom to get around the golf course and really get back to the game.

The toughest thing for me to accept about playing golf in this new way, was that I knew I would never be able to play as well as I had in the past. This really bothered me a great deal until, one day, I realized that I should not look at how I used to play, but rather, how I play now and how much I could improve from that day on. Once I accepted this, I began to see improvement and felt much better.

As my skills continued to improve, I began to give trick shot exhibitions. The more I did, the more I wanted to do and I now had a challenge and a goal to strive for. I never thought that I could make a career of this, but I have now been doing my show successfully for 17 years. I have appeared in 49 states (Alaska being the only I have not yet been to) and I travel about 100,000 miles a year.

I was motivated to succeed, not by money or fame, but by the fact that if I succeeded, I would be able to continue doing the one thing I really love the most and that was to play golf again. I also enjoyed putting forth the effort because for me, the fun was in trying and I excelled in an area that at one point seem impossible for me to even think about. Today, I still face rejection in some areas. It hurts, but I try to put these experiences in perspective and use them as a learning tool.

As I look back, I am so glad that I had the love of golf in my heart and that I chose to hang in when times were the bleakest. Thanks for giving me this wonderful opportunity to be included in your book. I hope our paths cross in the near future.

Sincerely,

DENNIS WALTERS
DW/fgl

cobra
GOLF INCORPORATED

8991 SW Eighth Street
Plantation, Florida 33324
305/474-3350

In association with

JOSEPH F. BARLETTA

BUSINESSMAN

...is President and Chief Executive Officer of TV Guide, *the nation's most successful magazine.*

Joe Barletta is the president and CEO to *TV Guide*, the nation's largest magazine, which sells approximately 14 million copies per week in 117 editions. *TV Guide* is also the nation's most successful magazine by revenue count, according to *Advertising Age*, a trade publication.

Joe Barletta is also the President and CEO of Murdoch Magazines, which distributes for client companies over 26.5% of the nation's total magazine circulation. Both companies generate annual revenues of approximately 9 billion dollars. By anyone's standards, Joe has achieved enormous success.

I have learned that no one reaches the level of success that Joe has attained without coming face to face with rejection and adversity. Joe's letter, however, was not reflective of a great number of terrible times or tragic hindrances. In fact, Joe seemed to feel that his letter would be of little value to this book.

Clearly, although Joe has quite obviously experienced rejection and disappointments, he simply refused to view his challenges in that light. We are all subject to rejection in one form or another. Joe Barletta makes plain the simple fact that one's attitude makes the difference between failure and success.

JOSEPH F. BARLETTA
President
Chief Executive Officer

100 Matsonford Road, Bldg. 4
Radnor, PA 19088
Tel: (610) 293-8510
Fax: (610) 975-0645

1211 Avenue of the Americas
New York, NY 10036
Tel: (212) 852-7204
Fax: (212) 852-7214

Dear Andy:

Despite the significant honor, you've embarrassed me! Clearly, I don't belong alongside these magnificent stories of spirit and perseverance and courage and vision and self-reliance. In my career climb, I've encountered no storms that I can recall, only a few drizzles that simply motivated me to move on to better opportunities.

Here's a vignette I'll offer, if appropriate:

I participated in high school newspapers and yearbooks, and while at Marietta College (Ohio), I was news editor of the newspaper and sports editor of the yearbook. Also, while in college, I was a daily correspondent for a newspaper in Columbus and was a stringer for UPI. Then, after college, I was hired as a reporter for the local daily newspaper where I worked until military service intervened.

Some years later, I was graduated from law school with the goal of learning management labor law. I asked my friend who ran the county legal placement office to get me an interview with the leading law firm in the big city -- which had several Fortune 500 industrial companies as clients.

I was crushed when he said he'd get me a courtesy interview but the firm would not consider hiring a Catholic and certainly not an Italian-American.

For the next couple of years I tried unsuccessfully in Washington and Harrisburg to get a government job where I could learn labor law but I had no connections. Finally, I filed a resume with the American Bar Association placement service and I promised to go anywhere in the United States and work for any law firm or company where I could learn labor law.

This led to an interview where I was hired by Dow Jones, publisher of the Wall Street Journal, and in a few years both ambitions had been joined. I was considered to be one of the leading specialists in management labor law in the newspaper industry.

From that serendipitous beginning, my career has been a glorious gift and has seen me living on Michigan Avenue, Fifth Avenue, Russian Hill, California's Riviera and Philadelphia's Main Line.

Today I am entrusted with the management of the biggest magazine in the United States, enjoyed every week by forty million readers. In addition, I have a front row seat as the greatest media adventure in the history of the world is conducted by the man who brought me here -- Rupert Murdoch.

Andy, none of this would have been possible if that law firm had been willing to hire me!

Cordially,

Joe B.

DALE EVANS ROGERS

ACTRESS/AUTHOR

...is one of the entertainment world's favorite authors and is now working on her twenty-fifth book. Dale and husband, Roy, have been featured on the covers of such magazines as Time *and* Life.

When I was six years old, I <u>was</u> Roy Rogers! I could walk like him, talk like him - I even tried to yodel. I wore plastic, pearl handled cap guns, a bright red cowboy hat and rode a stick horse named "Trigger." At six years old, I was certain the only girls who didn't have cooties were my mother and Dale Evans. She was a cowgirl who could sing and ride with the best of them.

But off the screen, Dale Evans is even a truer representation of a wholesome American lady than motion pictures could ever portray. The next time your child sings "The Bible Tells Me So," think of Dale Evans. She wrote it. Dale began her acting career by first displaying her talent for singing and song writing and continued by starring in several western movies with her husband Roy.

Dale is an accomplished author who has published over 25 books. This includes her highly acclaimed *Angel Unaware*. Dale Evans has been well aquainted with sorrow in her life, and yet, she holds her head high with hope for the future. Dale Evans has always been, and continues to be, an inspiration. After all these years of her fine example, we still need her now more than ever.

Roy Rogers — Dale Evans Museum

15650 Seneca Road, Victorville, California 92392
(619) 243-4547

Roy Rogers   Dale Evans Rogers

Dear Andy:

Everyone experiences failure at some time in life. Failure is not as important as the attitude we take toward it.

Each one of us has been endowed with special talents, abilities, personalities, and a free will given by our Great Creator.

There have been failures in my life . . . wrong choices, taking the wrong way at the fork in the road. However, I have experienced great happiness, much sorrow, and a measure of achievement by the Grace of God, to whom I have committed my life in the spring of 1948, shortly after my marriage to Roy Rogers.

When I was a child, I wanted to become a writer, a singer, a painter, and a ballerina.

In high school I loved writing essays, short stories, and made good marks in English. In my teens my heart was in music and composing songs. I submitted one of my songs to a music publisher, knowing nothing about copyrights. A few months passed, with no news from the publisher, one day in a "variety store" looking through their sheet music there was my song, bearing the name of another writer -- the same song, slightly altered. I was "down but not out."

Working for an insurance company as secretary to the claim adjuster, my boss caught me dabbling with lyrics to a tune of mine, instead of typing his claim forms. He invited me to play and sing on a radio show in which he was involved as a singer. This opened the way for me to get my own program.

During the "Great Depression" in the early thirties, I tried to break into radio in Chicago, but finally wound up as a stenographer for Goodyear Tire & Rubber. However, my heart was still in music and song writing.

I sang on WHAS in Louisville, Kentucky; WFAA in Dallas, Texas; and with dance bands. Finally, when I was on the staff at WBBM, a Chicago CBS outlet, I was summoned to Hollywood for a screen test. I had written a Leap Year song entitled "Will You Marry Me, Mr. Laramie?" which landed me a screen contract at 20th Century Fox.

After a year at Fox, I completed 39 weeks on the Chase & Sanborn Hour with Edgar Bergen. During that time, Republic Studios hired me on a year's contract.

Roy Rogers and I married on December 31, 1947. We had made 26 western pictures together. One month after our marriage, I committed my life to God through Jesus Christ. I prayed that He would use my life in any way He saw fit. When we married, I had a son; Roy had an adopted daughter, his own daughter and a 15-month-old baby boy, whose mother had died shortly after his birth.

Roy and I later had a little girl. Our Robin Elizabeth, a Downs Syndrome baby. She lived two years. Two days after her burial, God gave me the message of "Angel Unaware," which book is now in the 29th printing and considered a classic in religious literature. Finally, my writing came into play from the anguish of a mother's heart.

Dr. Norman Vincent Peale offered to write the forward and Angel Unaware was launched by Fleming H. Revell in the spring of 1953, appearing on the New York Times Best Seller list for many weeks.

During our television western series, I was asked to write a little Sunday school type song to be sung by a young girl in the episode. I said a prayer and in less than an hour "The Bible Tells Me So" was done. When that show aired, NBC and our sponsor said the song was too religious and must be deleted for rerun. However, Don Cornell, on Lucky Strike's Hit Parade requested permission to record it. His record connected with public fancy and became a hit. The network and sponsor said they would reinstate it on our reruns.

I decided Roy should have a "trail song" for his sign-off on the Mutual Radio Network radio show, and one afternoon I wrote "Happy Trails" in about three hours. No one was more surprised than I when "Happy Trails" took off with the public.

My hardest tribulations came with the loss of our Robin Elizabeth, the death of our adopted Korean-Puerto Rican daughter, Debbie, our adopted Kentucky-born son, Sandy, and grandson, Mark Rose. However, the Bible says "God giveth and God taketh away; blessed be the name of the Lord." We are blessed with six children, 15 living grandchildren, and 30 great-grandchildren.

My credo is: never, never give up; say "yes!" to tomorrow!

Thank you, Andy, for asking!

Sincerely,

DALE EVANS ROGERS

DER/jlh

*"We grow great by dreams.
All big men are dreamers."*

Woodrow Wilson

DON JAMES

FORMER HEAD COACH
WASHINGTON HUSKIES

...became the Winningest Coach in Pac-10 history in 1988. Don has been inducted into the Rose Bowl Hall of Fame.

One of the most uncomfortable and humbling experiences a person can endure is... change. But the person who is strong enough to humble himself for the sake of positive change will inevitably attain great personal growth and satisfaction.

Don James is the former head football coach of the University of Washington Huskies. He had enjoyed amazing success as a college football coach. Don was "coach of the year" on more than one occasion and had taken his team to 10 bowl games. In 1988, he was honored as the winningest coach in Pac 10 history. Don knew how to coach a football team.

But then came a stunning season of losses. Don James did not shirk his accountability. He was a strong enough person to open himself to the idea of changing his own methods rather than blaming outside factors for the breakdown.

Don stresses the need to set specific goals in order to exceed your own personal best with each effort, and not concern yourself with "attaining it all" immediately. Don's personal accountability to himself and his team allowed him to change for the better - so did the Washington Huskies football team, who got back on its pace as the team to beat!

NATIONAL CHAMPIONS 1991
Defending Rose Bowl Champions 1991, 1992

Dear Andy;

When I received an invitation to put in writing some thoughts about my career, my first thought was that it would be fun, and secondly, it hopefully might be of some value to a person facing disappointment and adversity.

As the head coach of the University of Washington Huskies, we had enjoyed very good success through my first 12 seasons. We had been in nine straight bowl games, ten in all. This included three Rose Bowl games, and one Orange Bowl. Then in 1988, we went 6-5 with one of our more experienced teams. We lost five games by a total of 15 points and although many teams would have been proud of this effort, I was NOT. Our fans and alumni were not too happy either.

When you lose in a visible sport such as football, you get quite alot of criticism. Some people want to credit this criticism for our turnaround. I do not believe that for one minute.

I was being accused of many things, some of which were: the game had passed me by....I could not relate to the modern day athlete...I was the most overrated coach in the Pac 10....and on it went.

I realized some changes had to be made but I also knew that you win football games with good fundamentals...in other words...if you do not block and tackle, you do not succeed. In our attempt to turn things around, I categorized the areas that needed to be improved.

I dealt with our staff...our recruiting process...our players...and...our style of football.

STAFF....I let one coach go. I was determined to get all coaches more involved with the athletes off the field and be more positive in our coaching.

RECRUITING...Our system was good, but we had some coaches that tried to take short cuts. In other words, we brought in too many players that were either not talented enough, fast enough or were not committed to becoming as good as they possibly could become.

SQUAD MEMBERS...I met with all returning players and asked them what they felt we must do to improve their group; i.e. linebackers, defensive backs, defensive line, running backs, quarterbacks, kickers etc. Then I asked them to list two things that they needed to do to improve.

1993 Rose Bowl

1992 Rose Bowl

1991 Rose Bowl

1989 Freedom Bowl

1987 Independence Bowl

1986 Sun Bowl

1985 Freedom Bowl

1985 Orange Bowl

1983 Aloha Bowl

1982 Aloha Bowl

1982 Rose Bowl

1981 Rose Bowl

1979 Sun Bowl

1978 Rose Bowl

UNIVERSITY OF WASHINGTON DEPARTMENT OF INTERCOLLEGIATE ATHLETICS
Don James, Head Coach (206) 543-2242
Dick Baird, Recruiting Coordinator (206) 543-2292

D.V. "Tubby" Graves Building, GC-20, Seattle, Washington 98195 FAX (206) 543-5000

I then changed our goal setting approach. We focused in on each athlete setting new personal records. We listed their best strength and lift tests, their speed and quickness tests, and said that each quarter of school we wanted to get as many P.R.'s as we could. Example: If you can lift 200 pounds in the bench press, let's shoot for 210 this work-out period. What it did for us was the players stopped fretting if they could not lift 300-400 pounds....they worked on their own personal best record.

We were amazed as coaches as to how much stronger and faster we became as a team with this approach.

FOOTBALL...On offense we felt as though we had some good young quarterbacks and receivers and we wanted to open up our offense. On defense we wanted to be more attacking and aggressive as we developed quickness and speed.

These changes helped the players and the coaches became more committed and this led to four more Bowl games, three of them back to back Rose Bowls plus a 12-0 season and a national title.

I strongly believe that if we had not had the disappointing 1988 season, we would not have had made the changes to get to another higher level of competition.

Sincerely,

Don James

Don James

*"Dream no small dreams,
for they have no power to
move the hearts of men."*

*Johann Wolfgang
Van Guethe*

MIKE ERUZIONE

OLYMPIC GOLD MEDALIST

...was the enthusiastic captain that led the 1980 United States Olympic Hockey Team to its Gold Medal Victory at Lake Placid.

I have always been an avid fan of the Olympics. The Olympic games bring out the best in the world's greatest athletes. The Olympic arena is a place where dreams have been fulfilled and hearts have been broken, but it is a stage to the world and it is always awe inspiring.

Certainly, the American hockey team of the 1980 winter games was one of the most memorable and inspirational Olympic teams our nation has exhibited in this century. They weren't expected to contend for a medal of any sort. The competition was too stiff. Hockey wasn't America's game anyway. There was no chance.

These are the things everyone seemed to be telling the US Hockey team captain, Mike Eruzione. But with undaunted spirits and a willingness to conquer what seemed impossible odds, Mike and his teammates picked up their sticks with a firm resolve. They were to become a team of destiny. They played with their hearts. They would show what Americans were made of - grit, determination and an enduring faith in their dreams. The gold medals they won speak with power of the relentless pursuit of those dreams that stunned the world. They made us proud to be Americans and taught us all a lesson worth remembering... Never give up!

Boston University

Mike Eruzione
Director of Special Programs
Office of Alumni Relations
19 Deerfield Street
Boston, Massachusetts 02215
617/353-5261
Fax: 617/353-5838

Andy Andrews
P.O. Box 2761
Gulf Shores, Alabama 36547

Dear Andy,

As I write this letter I can't recall ever considering that our 1980 U.S. Olympic Hockey Team *couldn't* win a medal. On the other hand, I can't recall ever thinking that it was a sure thing, either. What stands out in my mind is that, going into the Olympics that year, none of the "experts" thought we had a shot. In fact, our U.S. team was scarcely mentioned in the pre-Olympic press coverage.

But being virtually ignored in the press was not a big deal to us. Our real test of belief and confidence actually came right before the Olympic Games. We had been traveling across the country playing against teams everywhere. We thought we were pretty good. Then we played the Soviet Team in our last exhibition game before the Olympics. They beat us *bad*. 10 to 2 was the final score. We could have said, "Oh boy, we'll never beat that team. Look how good they are and how bad we are." But we didn't do that. Instead we got together and decided that the next time we met that team we would be better prepared mentally and physically than they were. We went to work. We knew that we had prepared well over the past six months and that our goal was set. The game the Soviets won 10 to 2 didn't count. It was a lifetime away, in the past, and had nothing to do with the task at hand...winning an Olympic medal for the U.S.

We went to the Winter Olympics and began winning. And with each win our confidence grew as we began to realize how close we were to accomplishing our goal. Then came the inevitable game with the same Soviet team that had embarrassed us just two weeks before. We had no idea what the outcome would be. I'd like to say, "Oh yeah, we knew going in that we had it in the bag," but we didn't know anything except that we were going to play every second as hard as we could. And, as it turned out, that's how we won.

Several little plays added up to one great victory. Mark Johnson's goal with one second left in the first period allowed us to go in tied 2-2 instead of trailing... Jim Craig came up with some great saves for us...positive things began happening and after falling behind 3-2 we were able to tie it at 3-3. Then I scored the go-ahead goal. All these things added up to keep us in the game, keep us believing we had a chance to win this thing. As the game played out every player on the team increased his intensity. When we were on the bench watching out teammates playing their hearts out it made us want to get in there and do even more. It was like the flu bug. It got around the room into everybody and made us want to play hard for each other. Of course we won that game, and that is what most people remember...but that game didn't win the Gold.

What most people have forgotten is that we had to play Finland 2 days later. If we'd lost to Finland, there was a chance we'd have come in fourth. There's no medal for fourth place. So, we didn't go to the Olympics to beat the Soviets. We went to win a medal for the U.S.A. So, instead of letting down and losing focus, we knew we had to keep our game face on and finish the job. I'm happy to say we were able to finish the job and bring home the Gold.

I believe the reason for our success can be summed up in one word. *Work.* The entire 1980 U.S. Olympic Hockey Team was made up of guys from working class, lunch pail, hard hat families that taught us the value of work. Our victory wasn't a miracle, it wasn't a fluke and it wasn't luck. It was the result of hard work to accomplish something most people thought we couldn't do. Certainly some of the other teams had better technical skills than we did, but none had our work ethic and that made the difference. No matter what you do for a career, no matter what other people think of your chances, if you learn the value of work, you will be successful at some point in your life. Don't be afraid to go for your Gold!

Your friend,

Mike Eruzione

*"No matter what a
man's past might have been,
his future is spotless."*

John R. Rice

JACK LaLANNE

PHYSICAL FITNESS LEGEND

...is 81 years of age and still recognized as the premier founder of the physical fitness movement in America.

Jack LaLanne is the father of the modern health and fitness rage, and was ushering in this era years before it was in vogue. Long before Reebok, LA Gear and Norditrack were available, Jack was teaching people how to become fit with old fashioned determination and commitment to a healthy lifestyle.

Just as the resistance of the barbells caused his arms to grow strong, the rejection Jack faced caused his attitude and mental determination to become powerful. The more resistance and rejection he endured, the stronger he became as a person.

Jack's philosophies about physical fitness were once scoffed at. But, over time, they have born themselves out to be true. Jack LaLanne, now at an age most would call their "golden years," is still the epitome of vitality and energy. His attitude can be summed up with one of his work-out phrases, "Come on now, stay with it!"

from the desk of *Jack LaLanne*

P.O. Box 1023 San Luis Obispo, CA. 93406
(800) 328-5225 (805) 772-6000 (805) 772-2590 fax

Mr. Andy Andrews
P.O. Box 2761
Gulf Shores, AL. 36547

Dear Andy,

I am very honored and flattered that you have asked me
to tell my story in your book. I have faced many kinds of
rejection during my eighty plus years. However, the
beauty of living a long and successful life is being able
to overcome those rejections and use those experiences to
make your life more prosperous.

One of the very earliest rejections that I faced was
at the age of 15. My body was rejecting me because I
wasn't taking care of it properly. I was a full blown
sugaraholic and junk food junkie. I was nearsighted, had
boils and pimples, wore arch supports and endured painful
headaches. After I attended a health lecture by
nutritionist Paul Bragg I decided to change my ways and
begin exercising and eating healthy. This of course was
the beginning of my life long career in the physical
fitness business.

Even after this great new beginning to my life I still
endured the rejection of my peers. All of the kids at
school made fun of me because I was a strict vegetarian.
I didn't eat cakes, pies, cookies, ice cream, soda pop or
any refined grains. At the same time I was also working
out with barbells and dumbbells which they thought was
weird. I was constantly referred to as musclebound. The
girls wouldn't date me because they said I was a freak.
Even the school newspaper printed pictures that were meant
to make fun of me.

The rejection did not end there. When I opened my
first gym in 1936 everybody was against me. The doctors
said that working out with weights would give people heart
attacks, cause hemorrhoids and they would lose their sex
drive. They said that if women worked out they would look
like men. I had to conceal the fact that I had earned a
Chiropractic degree because the Doctors and the
Chiropractors did not agree with one another in those days

and I didn't want anyone to have any ammunition against me. Even the coaches didn't want their athletes working out with weights because they thought they would get muscle bound. People thought that I was a charlatan and a nut. I had to give some of my early students keys to the gym so that they could work out at night. To get people to come to my gyms I would put on a tight T-Shirt and go to the schools and pick out the fattest and the skinniest kids there and ask them if they wanted to get in shape. I would work with them and eventually their parents would see the progress that was being made and they too would come to my gyms so that they could get in shape.

Through all of this I continued to keep my spirits up and kept trying to get my point across. Why you ask? because I believed very strongly in what I was doing. eventually my theories were proven and now everybody is working out. Yesterday I was a nut and a charlatan, today I am an authority and still saying the same thing. I believe that anything in life is possible if you make it happen.

Healthfully yours,

Jack LaLanne

*"Be thou the rainbow
to the storms of life."*

George Gordon Byron

MANNIE L. JACKSON

ENTREPRENEUR

...is Chairman and owner of the Harlem Globetrotters. When he purchased the Globetrotters in 1993, he became the first African-American and former player to own a sports/entertainment organization.

Who among us has not watched the Harlem Globetrotters open mouthed and amazed at the impossible shots? As a piece of Americana, they are entrenched in our minds. Everyone loves the Globetrotters.

As an all-star basketball player in college, Mannie Jackson prepared himself for the pros. After a career in New York, Mannie played for the Globetrotters. The mental devotion and winning philosophy he reinforced then was drawn upon to see him through a coming storm.

Mannie now owns the Harlem Globetrotters and was the first African-American and former player to own a sports/entertainment organization. Mannie has succeeded personally by exercising his standards of excellence while facing obstacles.

Mr. Andy Andrews
P.O. Box 2761
Gulf Shores, AL. 36547

Mannie Jackson
Chairman

Dear Andy:

It was an honor to be chosen to be a part of "Storms of Perfection". As an African American, I have had many obstacles to overcome, but the one I will share altered my life and could have happened to anyone.

In the summer of 1969, I had just moved to Minneapolis from Detroit, Michigan and was beginning a career with the Honeywell corporation. In the back of my mind, I entertained the idea of going back into professional basketball. I was in shape, I always had been, having been an All Star at the University of Illinois and having had a professional career with New York and the world famous Harlem Globetrotters. My dreams were dashed by of all things, "the hiccups". The "hiccups" were caused by a ruptured diaphragm resulting from an altercation several years earlier in a Harlem Globetrotter game.

I was on summer break at my parent's home in Edwardsville, Illinois, when I started hiccuping. It seemed like normal hiccups, except that I continued for nearly 12 hours! I ended up in St. Louis University Hospital with pneumonia caused by the ruptured diaphragm. I was rushed into emergency surgery to repair my diaphragm. Four surgeries followed which resulted in my diaphragm being repaired and a portion of my stomach being removed along with surgery on the valve from my esophagus into my stomach. From my well conditioned 195 pound athletic body, after four months in the hospital, my 6'3" frame weighed only 95 pounds! I can vividly remember from my bed seeing family and friends come to visit and the look on their faces. I must have looked like death to them and on at least two occasions the doctors lost hope. However, even after seeing myself in the mirror, I really believed I could come back and play professional basketball again. Truly the power of positive thinking!

My mother was my "Rock of Gibraltar" during this time. She never missed a day driving one hour and a half to visit me in my hospital room that had become my whole world. With the unending support of my family and friends, and an optimistic attitude, I was able to make the transition from the hospital to my parent's home. There were a couple more hospital stays due to complications. All in all, I spent almost a year recovering from surgeries and hospitalizations.

Harlem Globetrotters International, Inc. • 6121 Santa Monica Blvd. • Hollywood, California 90038 • (213) 468-0280 FAX (213) 468-0292

333 So. 7th Street, Suite 2880, Minneapolis, MN 55402 • (612) 338-2102 FAX (612) 338-2409

Harlem Globetrotters International, Inc., A Division of MJA, Inc.

It was during these experiences - which were often spiritual; I realized the power of the human mind - Despite medical reports to the contrary - I never lost my will to live and to be productive or my belief that I would make a total come back. I learned to appreciate what really matters in life. I learned not to take my health for granted again. I never played professional basketball again, but I learned to re-focus and I dedicated myself to my family and my professional career. I realized that I was in charge of what happened in my life and that I had been given a second chance. I have since finished a great career with Honeywell, becoming a Senior Vice President and an Officer of a Fortune 500 corporation. I have several business interests and I am the Chairman and majority owner of the world famous Harlem Globetrotters.

I consider "obstacles" only as something to be gotten over. As we have all heard before, life is 10% what happens to us and 90% of how we react to it. Good luck with this and future projects, Andy -- you have the right attitude.

Warm Regards,

Mannie L. Jackson
Chairman

"A word aptly spoken is like apples of gold in settings of silver."

Proverbs 25:11

JEFFREY KRUGER

CONCERT PROMOTER

...is a 40 year veteran elder statesman of the British show business scene. He was the first promoter to launch the British rock'n roll industry.

I was fishing in a small river one afternoon a number of years ago. It was mid-spring and the water was rushing. A little way down stream, I could see a very large boulder, about the size of a small house, in the middle of the stream. I watched the white water crash against the rock and continued to flow around both sides.

I thought of that stream and equated it to the course of our lives and the boulder as a representation of situations and challenges we face from time to time. Certainly, the boulder was immovable. It was hard and the water was soft. But the water was flexible and able to seek a new course around it. The water was not dammed up to become stagnant. Its bending, adaptable qualities allowed it to continue at full speed, full of beauty and life. I could see the marks of erosion on the rock and knew that over the course of time, that soft, flexible, adaptable current would one day dissolve that hard, immovable boulder into tiny grains of sand.

Jeffrey Kruger's first love was the piano. He saw the course of his life taking him to the fulfillment of his dream as a pianist. Then a boulder got in his way. Jeffrey was as flexible as a stream. He created success from failure. He has promoted to the public bands and entertainers on a grand scale. Jeffrey Kruger is responsible for putting the British rock and roll industry in the public's eye. The boulders and other challenges were plentiful, but not so abundant as his hope and persistence!

T﹦K﹦O

Mr Andy Andrews,
P O Box 2761,
Gulf Shores, AL 36547
U S A

Dear Andy

May I initially congratulate you for the very excellence of the the two volumes of 'Storms of Perfection' which I have only just had the pleasure of reading. What a jolly good idea!

When I was 21, I was a frustrated Pianist who wanted to make piano playing the base for my future career. After hearing a recording by my friend to be, Erroll Garner play his composition 'Penthouse Serenade', I realised I could never be in that class and I decided to become a Promoter Entrepreneur and work with great artists by promoting their talents from the other side of the piano.

I looked around and found, that for young British people of my own age there was a need for opportunities to meet new friends, of both sexes, and I decided to promote a high class, top drawer Celebrity dance evening. This was to be my first real step in becoming the new British Sol Hurock, who as you know was the great American Impresario.

I booked one of the top British bands of the period plus a guest visit by a new, then upcoming vocal star and a second headliner who was another house hold name on the British music scene in 1952. All the ingredients were there - a unique event - a major venue - three top star names and a hoop - a - la promotional campaign to let everyone know that the event was forthcoming. I expected a minimum of 2000 dancers and being inexperienced, I was already figuring the massive profit I would make.

What a lesson for a budding promoter of future World talents!

I had aimed my campaign at the mainly Jewish teen and early twenty year old demographic audience, who at that time were starved of the chance of attending such a star studded get together.

THE KRUGER ORGANISATION, INC
P.O.BOX 130 . HOVE EAST SUSSEX BN3 6QU
Telephone: (44) 273 550088   Telefax: (44) 273 540969

I had previously run, very successfully I might add, very much smaller dances in clubs and always with great success with a similar format. However, I did not do ALL my homework research. Without thinking, the date I booked for the affair was, of all days, the first evening of the most High Holy Day in the Jewish religious calender, the eve of Yom Kippur.

The end result - 200 people and a massive loss of money & ego. It brought me down to earth and reality. After this I became known as the most meticulous collector of data applicable to each future act I was to promote ensuring I double checked every detail down to the smallest item such as even checking that the colour scheme in the hotel room would not offend them and changing the colour as necessary.

Since through the years I have successfully promoted concerts in many countries of the world with such super stars as Rudolf Nureyev, Martha Graham Ballet Troupe & Placido Domingo; from Jack Benny, George Burns & Wayne Newton to Julio Iglesias & Anne Murray; from The Jacksons to Gladys Knight & the Pips; from Marvin Gaye to Billie Holiday & Sarah Vaughan and then Isaac Hayes & Barry White; from Glen Campbell to Johnny Cash to Kris Kristofferson to Nitty Gritty Dirt Band & Brenda Lee to Nanci Griffith; from the early years of Led Zeppelin to Pink Floyd to Iron Maiden to Chuck Berry & Bill Haley & His Comets to signing new comers as The Moody Blues & David Bowie to music publishing contracts, I have learnt from this valuable lesson of failure and gone forward with renewed confidence and ability.

Good luck with the new book of which I am very proud to have been asked to be a part.

Sincerely,

Jeffrey Kruger

"The poorest of men is not the man without a cent; it is the man without a dream."

Anonymous

MARY ANN MOBLEY COLLINS

FORMER MISS AMERICA/ ACTRESS

...starred opposite Elvis Presley in "Girl Happy" and "Harum Scarum." Mary Ann has had the same home, the same telephone number, and the same marriage for 26 years.

With her intelligence, beauty and concern for the underprivileged, Mary Ann Mobley Collins was first brought to national attention as Miss America. She has continued throughout her life to be an honorable representation of our country. Mary Ann is truly a woman of many talents and accomplishments. It would seem that a person would not have enough time or energy to become so well versed in such a variety of endeavors.

She is an actress, who portrayed Maggie McKinney Drummond on the hit TV series "Different Strokes," Dr. Beth Everdeen on "Falcon Crest," and Mary Fran Smithers on "Hearts Afire." She has co-hosted the Miss America pageant with her husband Gary Collins. Mary Ann is a daredevil performer of death-defying circus acts, a scuba diver, an avid horsewoman, a documentary film producer, a charity fund raiser and a public speaker.

Mary Ann frequently visits third world countries to film documentaries and encourage assistance for millions of children and helpless victims of drought and war.

Mary Ann Mobley Collins has done all of this and much more while afflicted with an incurable intestinal disease. But you see, Mary Ann has always had a heart condition as well. She has conditioned her heart to give of herself no matter the challenges she faces, enriching others while finding herself healthier in the process.

Mr. Andy Andrews
P.O. Box 2761
Gulf Shores, AL 36547

Dear Andy,

Thank you so much for the opportunity to share with your readers a
part of my life that very few people know about.

There was a time in my career when I thought that life could not get
any better. I had just won the Golden Globe Award for "Most Promising
Newcomer", and I had signed a five year contract with MGM. I had just
completed my second movie with Elvis Presley, and had also made a
movie for CBS with Ingmar Bergman. Things were going very well indeed.

Suddenly, I was stricken with Crohn's Disease. This is an incurable
disease that attacks the intestines. Andy, I became extremely ill.
So much so that I began to doubt if I would ever again lead a normal
life. So many doubts crept through my thoughts... could anyone ever
love me knowing I had this terrible illness? Would I ever be able
to have a family?

I didn't want to talk with anyone about my illness. I even managed to
keep it a secret from the industry. Only once did I ever have to turn
down work because of my illness.

The turning point of my life came when I found a doctor who became a
partner and friend in my belief that I could overcome this disease, or
at least live with it with dignity. I have now been in remission for
20 years. I believe it is because God and I joined in the battle with
the help of this wonderful doctor against this horrible disease.

I am now a spokesperson for the Crohn's and Colitis Foundation of
America. I cherish the experiences I have had and the people I have met.
I truly believe that God does not close one door, without opening up
another.

I always try to remember the words of Emerson when he wrote... "To leave
the world a bit better, whether by a healthy child, a garden patch or a
redeemed social condition; to know even one life has breathed easier
because you have lived. This is to have succeeded."

Sincerely,

MARY ANN MOBLEY COLLINS

JOHN W. THOMPSON

ENTREPRENEUR

*...at the age of 18 he survived a
farm accident which severed
both of his arms.*

Society may lead one to believe that happiness and success falls upon those who are predestined to receive it. You may have heard it said, "Success breeds success, the rich get richer and the poor get poorer." I have little use for such expressions. As this letter from John Thompson reveals, great achievements don't magically seek out those that are naturally successful. Rather, they are forged from opportunities or necessity by those ordinary people with an extraordinary overcoming spirit. Not every famous person is necessarily a successful and overcoming person. The reciprocal is also true; not everyone who achieves great "miraculous" things are necessarily famous.

You may never have heard of John Thompson, but when I first learned of the tragedy that befell this young man and his amazing drive to defeat his challenges, I had to pursue a letter from him. Too many people, if put in John's situation, would have simply accepted their ill fate without attempting to make things better, believing that misfortune falls upon those predestined for it just as surely as favor and prosperity fall to those chosen for them.

The value in John's inspiring story is not found primarily in the end result of his recovery, but in his display of courage and his struggle to restore his own happiness. He refused to surrender and submit to his misfortune. John is a humble young man who would not call himself an inspiring example of accomplishment. His bravery and fortitude in the face of his adversity prove otherwise. John looked at his situation through the eyes of hope.

THOMPSON
ENTERTAINMENT

JOHN W. THOMPSON

226 WEST SWEET AVENUE, #1
BISMARK, ND 58504
701/258-6228

Mr. Andy Andrews
P.O. Box 2761
Gulf Shores, AL 36547

Dear Andy,

I thought long and hard about writing a letter to you for a book which includes so many people who are well know, famous, successful individuals. I am famous only for a nearly life ending, traumatic (and certainly preventable) accident.

It was a typical winter day, cloudy, snowy, in the 20 degree range and I was unloading barley from the truck into an auger to feed the hogs when my shirt got caught in the machinery. As I tried to free myself, the equipment grabbed my arms and spun my entire body around the auger shaft five or six times until my arms literally came off and I fell to the ground, unconscious. I don't know how long I lay there, but what woke me up was my blue heeler hound dog licking my face. I remember seeing that my arms were missing but not fully realizing what had happened. Then I stood up and the reality hit me. I screamed and my brain simply went on automatic. The pain center shut down and *something* took me through the steps necessary to survive. I remember the 400 foot walk to the house, opening the door to the house and then to the office using my head and then picking up a pencil with my mouth to dial an ambulance, but it was as though someone else was doing it for me. The ambulance team recovered my arms, packed them in ice and brought them to the hospital to attempt reattachment. Since then I have been through 16 operations in several hospitals, extensive rehab and have broken practically every medical record in the book!

My family was so helpful doing *everything* for me during this rehabilitation that I didn't get a chance to fully recover until I moved to Bismarck, North Dakota on my own where I have been more or less forced to fend for myself. I was 18 years old when the accident occurred. I am now 21 and have the use of my arms once again.

From the instant my blue heeler hound licked my face and woke me, Andy, and the realization of what had happened to me struck home, I have never considered *not* recovering. The series of steps to get better actually started with the first step of the 400 foot walk to the house that day. I believe when we're faced with any tragedy, physical or emotional, taking the steps one after another and not even considering failure will get you where you want to be.

Sincerely,

John W. Thompson

John W. Thompson

SUE MYRICK

CONGRESSWOMAN

...was the Republican Mayor of Charlotte, NC, when she was overwhelmingly elected to Congress.

Sue Myrick has a consistent record of fighting intrusive government and tax and spend policies. She first gained national recognition through her accomplishments as a two-term mayor of Charlotte, NC, where she championed tougher sentencing for criminals and led the fight against illegal drugs. Sue was also instrumental in bringing the NFL's Carolina Panthers to Charlotte.

Since her victory in the 1994 elections, Sue Myrick has played an active role in the 104th Congress. Sue was named one of the members of the House transition team and was later drafted by her peers as a Freshman Class Liaison to the Leadership.

I have been privileged to know Sue and her husband Ed for the past two years. Her quick smile makes her an easy person to befriend, but her honesty, integrity and commitment to do what is right makes her a valuable leader for the United States. As president and CEO of Myrick Enterprises, Sue knows what is needed for business to survive and prosper. She will continue to be an advocate for reducing government involvement in the lives of America's hard working men and women.

Congress of the United States
House of Representatives
Washington, DC 20515

Mr. Andy Andrews
Post Office Box 2761
Gulf Shores, Alabama 36547

Dear Andy,

There is an old saying that goes, "the world will never meet you half way." Throughout my business and political career, I have found this statement to be true over and over again. Overcoming obstacles, both personal and professional, is an experience all people will have to go through if they want to live a life marked by success and achievement.

From December of 1991 through May of 1992, I ran unsuccessfully for the Republican nomination for a seat in the United States Senate. In this my first run for statewide office, I faced a crowded field of four opponents. Though I had been a two-term mayor of Charlotte, North Carolina's largest city, my main opponent enjoyed greater statewide name recognition and an overwhelming spending advantage. Faced with these obstacles, I ran a common-sense campaign that emphasized face-to-face voter contact and home-style grassroots campaigning. I toured the state and met with voters, editorial boards, reporters and just regular "folk."

Unfortunately, just as most political campaigns inevitably turnout, this campaign was marked by periods of name-calling and false innuendos. Night after night I took the full brunt of my opponent's accusations that appeared on paid campaign television commercials, and those that were spread by word-of-mouth. Strapped for cash, I was unable to respond to these accusations and, therefore, was never able to let the voters know about the true "Sue Myrick."

On election night, I finished second in the race, having garnered a 30% return statewide. Many people thought my political career was over after that election, and in fact, I did take a two year hiatus from the political arena. But in 1994, not liking the direction our country was headed, I was elected to represent North Carolina's Ninth Congressional District in the United States House of Representatives.

I know today that I am a stronger person because of the Senate race. It was a lesson in humility and character development. Stung by the defeat, I was comforted in knowing that I had run a race of "integrity." I learned from that race that winning or losing is not necessarily defined by the final vote tally. Elections come and go, but integrity endures.

Sincerely,

Sue Myrick
Member of Congress

"History has demonstrated that the most notable winners usually encountered heart-breaking obstacle before they triumphed. They won because they refused to become discouraged by their defeats."

B.C. Forbes

ANNA CHENNAULT

AUTHOR

...is known internationally as an author having over 45 books published in English and Chinese. She holds numerous political affiliations to her credit.

As a boy, I remember watching the movies about World War II. I'd run across my backyard as fast as I could go - with my arms extended - trying to reproduce the sound of awesome engines and fury of battle. America's fighter pilots were my heroes. I thought the men who flew these machines were more than mortal and must have led lives beyond things so normal as families, wives and children. I would not realize until much later that my heroes were shaped, upheld and motivated to a great degree by the wives and families they loved.

Many know of General Claire Lee Chennault of Flying Tiger fame. His wife Anna was lesser known, but her tragedy epitomizes the circumstances of many young women in our society today: she was widowed and parted from the husband she had built her world around. She was consequently made a single mother of two children and found herself in a new and different place. Anna was unemployed and uncertain about making a life on her own. By the effort she put forth early in her career, learning to ignore rejection, she reaped success with her writing talent.

This propelled Anna into a myriad of successful ventures - author, diplomat, journalist and national advisor to US Presidents. Anna has outmaneuvered the hardships, common to many, which too often defeat the spirit of those unwilling to hope.

$\mathcal{CIC}$, $\mathcal{Inc}$.

Chennault Building 1049 30th. Street, N.W. • Washington, D.C., 20007 • Tel: 202 333 5921 • Fax:202 347 0373
CIC, Inc.. is a non-political, non-profit (501-(c)(3) organization working outside of governments to promote international goodwill.

ANNA C. CHENNAULT
Chairman

Andy Andrews
P. O. Box 2761
Gulf Shores, AL 36547

Dear Andy:

When I read through the 2 volumes of " STORMS OF PERFECTION ", I recognized many names and faces. Some of them have shared platforms with me as Public Speakers. Baby, I have come a long way!

This year, 1995, on Tuesday January 24th, in the Nations Capital, I was invited to the House Chambers to listen to President Clinton's address to a sharply partisan Congress. In the past, although I was very fortunate to have a seat (which has always been very difficult to get due to the limited seating), but this special night, I was personally escorted by the most senior Senator, Strom Thurmond of South Carolina to my seat in the Gallery. My late husband, General Claire Lee Chennault, would have been very proud of me. Yes, I have come a long way!

I first arrived in Washington, D. C. as a young widow, a young Chinese women in a strange land, among strange people, alone, with very little money and very few friends, and with two small children who needed my care and support. My husband, General Chennault, who was 33 years older than I, had just died of cancer, and I was totally unprepared to carry on a life on my own. It was one of the darkest periods of my time, my life.

I was born in Beijing, China, raised in a family of Chinese scholars and diplomats. As a young child, I enjoyed the life of a happy family filled with education and social distinction of the Chinese upper class, until the Japanese invasion forced our family flight to Hong Kong, and as a refugee student, I went with my school to interior China--Guangdong, Guangxi and Yunnan. When I finished college, WW II was over and I took a job as a young reporter with the famous Central News Agency. At the age of fifteen, I had published my first book and I was quite sure of myself as a young female reporter among men, working in Shanghai, China.

Meeting General Chennault change my whole life. A life that I didn't expect, and had to overcome so much hardship. We were married 2 days before Christmas,

43

1947. We overcame our age difference of 33 years, and our cultural difference, to live and work together. He, as the founder and Chairman of a new airline in Asia, Civil Air Transport, and I as a writer and public relations officer of his airline and editor of the airline's monthly magazine. Life with General Chennault was not an ordinary life, because he was always a fighter, fighting for the right cause, at that time, Communism in Asia and the Soviet Union. But our short years together were happy and full of challenge.

According to experts, marriages between persons of the same race, religion, age group and general background succeed far more often than others. Because our marriage lacked every one of these compatibility factors, we had to consul only our hearts and our minds. Our happy days and years did not last very long. In 1957, after his annual medical checkup at the Army Walter Reed Hospital in Washington, D. C., they announced that he had cancer and had to operated on as soon as possible. How could I ever forget that moment, and the time when I visited him before his operation. The following is part of his letter to me, hand written, the night before surgery:
" Dearest Little One,
I have no doubt that I will survive the operation tomorrow and live for many years with you and our beloved daughters. However, as you know, all things are in the hands of the Supreme Being and no one can know when he will be called back to the place whence he came.
If it should happen that I cannot see or be with you in the flesh again, I do want you to know and remember that I shall always be with you and the girls in the spirit. I love you and them as much as anyone can love and I believe love will endure beyond the grave.
Do remember and teach our girls the true principles of life-to be moral, to be honest, loyal and kind to all who need kindness. Live within your means, envy no one, enjoy both the comforts and the privation of life on this earth. Be humble and work hard at anything you choose for a profession... "

I found the rest of the words hard to read through my tears. I have read it many times since then, but the last words always blur.

For three interminable hours, he was on the operating table while they removed most of his left lung. For me it was three hours of purgatory. Finally the chief surgeon, Colonel Moncrief, came out of the operating room. I stood watching his face, tense and fearful to speak.

"He will be all right."
I swayed with relief and the doctor put his hand on my shoulder.
"I'm all right-now." I said to him.
I moved forward as the nurses wheeled the General out, on the way to the recovery room. His still features were almost the color of the sheet that covered him to chin.
My darling," I thought in anguish, " what have they done to you!"
Three days passed before they let me talk to him. I held his hands and tears wet my cheeks.
"Darling, why are you crying? I'll be all right," he said.
" I know, dear. I know."
For two days we waited for the results of the laboratory tests. On September 1st, we knew. Malignant!! General Chennault died on July 27 1958.

It was a bad dream. No this wasn't a dream! At that time, I thought of Elizabeth Barret Browning, her poem of parting:

"How do I love thee. Let me count the ways. I love thee with breath, smiles, tears, with all my life; And if God choose, I shall but love thee better after death"

Now that my husband was gone, and I was alone, hard decisions had to be made. And I made it!

I arrived in Washington equipped with little knowledge about the United States. I needed a job, and found one with Georgetown University. But I knew there was much more to do than just working at a job. Each night when I returned home from work, I continued my writing, and I tried my hand at writing my first book in English, "A Thousand Springs" I finished it in one year in my spare time. It's the an autobiography of a marriage and the famous author Dr. Lin Yutang wrote in his introduction, and I quote " Many books have been written about General Chennault of the Flying Tiger Fame. Yet, this is a book in a class by itself. It is one of those rare books where the author has something very deep and very human and very sad and very beautiful to say and say it well. General Chennault is now in the clouds-he belongs in the clouds anyway-and his "Little Jade" (Madam Chennault is still on earth), and she looked at his portrait in her bedroom, and the memories of their love floated back, compelling and sweetly said, and being a writer, she just wrote about things, chips from her memories, the little things of life, with warmth and affection and tenderness, of their great, enduring love....

"The fact that the subject of this book is Claire Chennault adds luster to it , but in my mind is incidental. This is not intended as a full-bodied biography of General Chennault, yet in the end what comes out is the portrait of a man, indomitable and suffering, tough and tender, independent-minded, stubborn, yet essentially simple and unassuming. What the reader gets is, in addition to the real core of the story, their wedded love and Chennault sickness and death, so many glimpses into the war in China, the Flying Tigers, the 14th Air Force and vignettes of the author's own ancestral home and her wonderful grandfather, and Peking, Kunming and Shanghai...."

To the U. S. publishers, I was a newcomer, I was an unknown. I didn't have an agent. After three publishers wrote me kind letters of rejection, the forth one-Paul E. Eriksson, a small publisher called me long distant (I was in Taipei, Taiwan at the time to introduce one of my new books). Paul Eriksson said " Mrs. Chennault), I finished reading your script. I spent all night reading it. It's very moving. It will be a good book. I want to be your publisher. Please return to the U. S. as soon as you can so we can talk." All I could say was "Yes, Yes." "A Thousand Springs" first printing came out in 1962. Within a month my book became the best seller on the New York Times book list and lasted for six months. The eighth printing was published in November 1070. I was scheduled for speeches all over the United States. I went on to write "Chennault and the Flying Tigers", "The Education of Anna" (by Times Books 1980 and just recently both China and Taiwan published the "Collection of Anna Chennault Writings".

In 30 years, I have published 45 books all together. Many of them best sellers in Asia. How Did I do it? Hard work, patient and keep learning each day, and never give up hope. Even in the darkest hours, remember, there will always be a dawn. This is my "STORMS OF PERFECTION" to share.

Oh, by the way. A Ph.D. candidate from Washington University in St Louis, Ms. Catherine Forslund, is now doing her Doctoral Dissertation on Anna Chennault entitled " Women of Two Worlds. "

Warmest regards,

Anna Chennault

PAT WILLIAMS

BUSINESSMAN

...is Chief Operating Officer and General Manager of the Orlando Magic. He has authored over a dozen books.

Pat Williams is the CEO and General Manager of the Orlando Magic basketball team in Florida. He is widely recognized throughout the sports world as a consummate promoter and astute talent scout. His zany antics and endless imagination inspired the Magic's phenomenal success almost immediately. He is also considered one of this country's premier motivational and humorous speakers, who has authored books on inspiration and wit. You will find no mention of these things in Pat's letter.

Neither does he mention that he failed in his dream of being a professional baseball player. He began managing baseball teams in the '60's and finally moved into managing basketball teams by 1968. He married his wife Jill and they share 18 children together (14 of these are adopted).

What you will notice in Pat's letter is the condition of his heart; his ability to realize the things in life that are most important and to pour his soul into making those matters work. It is no great surprise that his notable, and secondary, success in his business naturally followed and blossomed based on this condition of the heart.

Mr. Andy Andrews
P.O. Box 2761
Gulf Shores, AL 36547

Dear Andy,

December 19, 1992, has come to be known in my house as "D" day. It was the day of the bomb, the surprise attack, the confrontation that would make or break my ten year marriage.

Ironically, this "D" day was not planned. At age forty-two I was oblivious to the despair that had driven my thirty three year old wife to the brink. As far as I was concerned I had a nice normal marriage, and normal was fine with me. Normal was killing Jill.

As long as I live Andy, I will never forget these words..."I just don't care anymore" Jill said, so quietly that I almost didn't hear her. Almost, "I hate this marriage. It was boring me to death." I heard that as if she had screamed it in my ear, yet she spoke just above a whisper, staring at the floor. I leaned close to look in her face, realizing she meant in that her eyes and ever her color signaled something in her that I had never encountered. This wasn't something I could apologize away something I could patch up...

I realized as I sat there that I had just seen my wife die emotionally. I was the scariest day of my life. I knew Jill as the girl God had picked out for me. At this point she had given up completely on our marriage. She said only that she was not going to leave because it would devastate the children. Also she knew that as a Christian divorce was not an option.

I prayed for a miracle.

As a collector of books I have over 3,000 in the house. I searched desperately to find one on marriage and family that I thought would help. I found nothing but froth. One night after searching until 3:00 in the morning. I gave up and climbed into bed. I laid there full of resolve but desperate for tangible help. Unable to sleep, I flipped on the light on the bedside table, and there on that table illuminated by the light, was a book Jill had bought and brought home over eight months before. It had rested there collecting dust. She hadn't even read it. I was unmarked and apparently unopened. <u>Love-Live for Every Married Couple</u> (Zondervan, 1980) by Ed Wheat, M.D.

One Magic Place ☆ Orlando Arena ☆ 600 W. Amelia ☆ Orlando, Florida 32801-1114 ☆ (407) 649-3200 (Switchboard)

Dr. Wheat called his prescription for a superb marriage a practical course of action "that is both uncomplicated and effective." He entitled it BEST because that was an acronym formed by what he called "four positive elements that will transform any marriage: Blessing, Edifying, Sharing and Touching." Dr. Wheat said you must concentrate on all four areas every day without fail. So, every day I thanked God for Jill. Every day I would praise her and build her up, giving her support and self confidence. I would share time, activities, interests, ideas, family goals and thoughts with Jill everyday! And to touch her, not just sexually, but to sit close to her, hold her hand, give her a hug, and to have eye contact with her whenever we were speaking. These things are so important and so many times neglected.

From the moment I began the BEST theory, I remember each day getting a little better. There was inconsistencies and sometimes it would seem we were back to square one. But I was motivated to keep going, without pushing her, to the point where we would build a new life together.

Now we have a framework to handle whatever difficulties come along, I know if Jill isn't happy, then I have failed to bless, edify, share, or touch, and I am driven right back to the fundamentals.

I never wanted the memories to those dark days to leave me. Not that I ever wanted to go through them again, I'd rather die. But I want the memory to always be there. That's why we will always celebrate December 19 as an anniversary in our home. It marks the death of a marriage that had to die to allow the birth of one that had to be born.

Blessings,

Pat Williams

"Character may be manifested in the great moments, but it is made in the small ones."

Phillip Brooks

DAVID E. SALZMAN

TV PRODUCER

...is co-Chief Executive Officer of Quincy Jones - David Salzman Entertainment. As a producer he is responsible for many of television and radio's most successful shows.

If you have ever sat down to relax in front of your television set and enjoyed such shows as "Dark Justice," the "Jenny Jones" talk show, "Sports Illustrated," "Life" and "People" network specials, you have David Salzman to thank. David has created, developed and produced many of television and radio's most successful shows. He also created the News Information Weekly Service (N.I.W.S.), which has been syndicated to 150 television stations and 50 foreign countries for the past 10 years.

David has been the recipient of several national awards for his many contributions to radio and television. He has a masters degree in mass communications from Wayne State University in Detroit.

As a husband for 25 years and the father of three children, David is a success story, but it was not an overnight success. He forged his own opportunities through his resolve, determination and superior winning attitude. David learned wisdom from his failures and patterns from his success.

Quincy Jones · David Salzman Entertainment

Mr. Andy Andrews
P.O. Box 2761
Gulf Shores, Alabama   36547

Dear Andy,

My lucky break came when I was nine and I just didn't
recognize it at the time. Growing up on the streets of
Brooklyn, sports was a way of life, but one day I found
myself the odd man out in a pickup baseball game. Neither
team wanted me.

I was devastated. A year before I was one of the best
fielders and hitters, though lately I had trouble catching
routine fly balls. That rejection unknowingly led to the
turning point in my life.

When I told my parents what happened they took me to a
doctor for a checkup. He found nothing. After another
examination I was asked to wait outside the doctor's office
and I overheard him tell my mother, "There's zero wrong, he's
just a nervous kid." My parents never bought that sad
diagnosis and kept on searching for an answer. One year and
ten doctors later it was discovered that I had polio.
Undetected, the disease had progressed and my whole left
side eventually suffered muscle spasms and atrophy.

Next I found myself as a regular outpatient at a hospital
for chronic diseases. I was among far more severely
stricken adults and children. A doctor put me in a youth
group and had us throw around a medicine ball. I noticed
that every guy in the group had accepted his fate as a
cripple. Thanks wholly to my parents and daily therapy for
a few years I overcame any paralysis. Further, I ended up a
better athlete than I would have been, not so much because
of the ambidexterity I learned, but because I recognized
early on that if you don't give up almost anything can be
accomplished.

3800 Barham Blvd. Suite 503 · Los Angeles, California · 90068
Telephone 213/874-2009 · Fax 213/874-3364

Page Two
Andy Andrews Letter

This life lesson, which started with peer rejection, made me stronger as a student and as a professional. I knew that there were far worse consequences than rejection. Like losing hope and admitting you'd rather quit than fight daunting odds.

So, when I ran for office in school and lost, didn't make a team, failed to be selected editor or got turned down for a date I was lucky to understand that it hurt but I'd survived far worse blows. And lots of other people faced much greater adversity.

When my high school guidance counselor told me I had virtually no chance of getting into the college of my choice I felt he might be right, however, I'd work doubly hard to prove him wrong. And somewhat to my own surprise, I did. He told me to lower my sights or risk suffering painful rejection. I say to everyone raise your sights, believe in yourself, set a goal and go all out to achieve it. If you do, that's great. If not, at least you can be satisfied you tried your best. Moreover, take from each disappointment, especially a near-miss, something positive and build on it. Next time you may win.

I tried three years to get a summer job as a copy boy at The New York Times. I knew nobody and nothing about how to accomplish this. The last day of hiring the third year, in desperation, I took the subway to the personnel office and waited there nine hours as every person but me got an interview. At closing time, the man who ran the summer program noticed me in the waiting room and said I looked so pathetic that I reminded him of himself at my age. With that opening I worked harder the next year and got the job. It paid $37.50 before taxes, yet it felt like a million dollars each day I went to work.

Page Three
Andy Andrews Letter

Perhaps I'm wrong but I believe that to stumble and bleed,
to believe and pursue, to overcome obstacles and naysayers,
to stand alone and fight for what is right, to be vanquished
and still persevere, to finally prevail and win with
humility is the noblest journey. There are no shortcuts or
easy roads. Those who have stared back at rejection and
proceeded with greater resolve are not only better equipped
to wear victory well but they are the ones most likely to
scale the loftiest peaks.

To this point a favorite Longfellow quotation comes to mind:

> "The heights by great men reached and kept,
> Were not attained by sudden flight.
> But they, while their companions slept,
> Were toiling upward in the night."

Sincerely,

David E. Salzman
Co-CEO, Quincy Jones-David Salzman Entertainment

DWAYNE HICKMAN

ACTOR

...recognized by most as "Dobie Gillis" from the television series "The Many Loves of Dobie Gillis." Dwayne played "Dobie" from 1959-1963.

Dwayne Hickman began his acting career at an early age, appearing in feature films before he entered his teens. As a sophomore at Loyola, he was asked by Bob Cummings to play the part of his nephew "Chuck" on "The Bob Cummings Show." This was the beginning of a 10-year stint on network television.

Most of us remember Dwayne as Dobie Gillis - a role he played from 1959 - 1963. This show delighted millions of viewers each week with the tales of Dobie and his girlfriends. The show is still popular on The Nickelodeon Network where it airs nightly.

Dwayne went on to become a program executive with CBS where he oversaw production of such shows as "M*A*S*H," "Designing Women" and "WKRP in Cincinnati." Dwayne and his wife Joan now live near the beach in Los Angeles with their proudest production, a son named Albert who was born on November 23, 1992.

DWAYNE HICKMAN

Mr. Andy Andrews
Post Office Box 2761
Gulf Shores, Alabama 36547

Dear Andy,

I would like to congratulate you on the success of your books, **"Storms of Perfection I & II"**, and I am very pleased that I have been asked to contribute to your third edition.

Last year my wife Joan and I co-authored my autobiography, **"Forever Dobie... The Many Lives Of Dwayne Hickman"**. I had to examine all the twists and turns my life has taken and I found this process to be thought provoking, embarrassing, insightful, and humorous. I would like to share with you a life changing moment.

When people hear the name Dwayne Hickman they usually remember me as "Dobie Gillis". The T.V. series "The Many Loves Of Dobie Gillis" chronicled the life of a teenage boy named "Dobie" who was the average American kid. In real life my childhood was anything but average.

My older brother Darryl was a child actor and my mother would drag me along to the studio when he was working. She hoped that I would follow in my brother's footsteps, but I was a shy and quiet kid who hated being the center of attention and longed to be "just another kid". Whenever I got a part as an extra I'd do my best to hide behind the scenery and melt into the crowd.

When I was 14, I made my stage debut in a play at the prestigious Pasadena Playhouse where my brother had the lead in a play called "This Young World". From the first day of rehearsals the tough talking woman who directed the play and I were like oil and water. She considered me an untalented kid and I thought she was more drill sergeant than director. Every day for weeks she'd go out of her way to embarrass and criticize me. At one point she threw up her hands in disgust and said, "Dwayne... I'm sick of watching you amble around the stage... You act like Gary Cooper!!" When I heard that all my feelings of intimidation suddenly evaporated. Maybe she didn't think much of Gary Cooper's acting prowess, but for a kid who never considered himself an actor I was thrilled by the comparison.

Finally opening night came and I nervously stood in the wings waiting for my cue. My big moment was a fight scene with my brother who played the town bully. Maybe it was the excitement of opening night or that he had a legitimate excuse to knock his little brother around, but suddenly I was taking a beating from my brother that was more like our brawls at home than what we had been rehearsing.

Page Two

This was no life for a kid... If I wanted to be miserable and get beat up I could have stayed home. I didn't need the humiliation of being on stage in front of seven hundred people.

The next night the reviews were passed around. The critics gave my brother his usual glowing reviews and the play was considered moderately entertaining. When I saw my name in the reviews and read the critics' comments I couldn't believe it. They said I was everything from dull, untalented, distractingly bad to uninteresting and amateurish.

I sat there looking at reviews that I considered very unfair... then suddenly something snapped inside of me. Instead of feeling embarrassed and upset, I was very angry. "Who were these guys anyway... I didn't care what they or anyone else thought." I had been doing the best that I could do in a situation I didn't want to be in. I had put up with the director criticizing every move I made, taken a public beating from my brother, and now these critics decided to unload on me.

It was at that moment my survival instinct kicked in... and since that night it has never left me. From that point on I decided that nobody was ever going to make me feel bad about myself again. I would never give that kind of power to anyone.

I have experienced many ups and downs personally and professionally. Whenever I get off-track and get caught up in a problem I stop myself and remember that 14 year old kid in his dressing room. I recall the determination and strong sense of survival I felt and suddenly I'm back in control.

Some of our most valuable lessons are learned in childhood and they can be called upon to give us strength and courage as we face the challenges of life.

Best regards,

DWAYNE HICKMAN

DH/fa

*"My mother said to me,
'If you become a soldier
you'll be a general; if you
become a monk you'll end
up as the pope.' Instead,
I became a painter and
wound up as Picasso."*

Pablo Picasso

MORT DRUCKER

CARTOONIST

...is known internationally for his caricatures, satirical movies, TV features and covers for MAD Magazine *for thirty-five years.*

After receiving Mort Drucker's letter, I began thinking about the hours I've spent thumbing through issues of *Mad Magazine*. The Mort Drucker cartoons were always my favorite, an opinion obviously shared by millions of people.

Here now is your chance to hear from the heart of Mort Drucker, one of the most prominent and zany cartoonists of all time whose works have been widely published by *Mad Magazine*. He has quite literally entertained several generations. Leaving home with the promise of great things to come, Mort's swift rejections only kindled his fire for success. His letter shows once again that there will always be people and problems standing in our way, but he gives sound advice as to what to do when faced with such encounters.

Mort Drucker's drawings can be found in the national portrait gallery of the Smithsonian Institution in Washington D.C. He has received the "Rueben Award" (the cartoonist's Oscar), from the National Cartoonist Society. He continues to create caricatures for *Mad Magazine* and has had a nationally syndicated political strip "Benchley" (retired in 1986). He has created TV features and has earned invitations to the White House. Mort recently illustrated the children's book *Whitefish Will Rides Again*.

IIIQꞧT·DRUCK∃R

Mr. Andy Andrews
P.O. Box 2761
Gulf Shores, Alabama 36547

Dear Andy:

For as long as I can remember I loved to draw, a compulsion undoubtedly the result of the "art gene" inherited from my grandfather who was a fine artist. All through school my parents and teachers encouraged this love and made me feel I had real talent. When I graduated high school I began to think of building a career in the art field. Not letting a lack of formal training deter me, I put together a portfolio. Full of confidence I crossed the river from Brooklyn to Manhattan, the Big Apple . . center of the universe for comic and cartoon artists.

My job hunt took me right to the offices of the N.Y. Daily News and the Daily Mirror. I was received with courtesy, evaluated with kindness and quickly shown the door. My rejection by two top papers was a rude welcome to the real world. I walked through Times Square that sunny afternoon feeling depressed, embarrassed and wondering if I really had talent. I wandered into a movie theater to hide out and seek solace in the darkness.

If anything rejection made me more determined to make a life in the art world. I also realized that to be a successful artist would require training and experience. Eventually I got a job as an apprentice to a syndicated cartoonist. That experience helped me step up to the next level. I became a staff artist for National Periodicals (now D.C. Comics), the largest comic book publisher. My job was to make editorial corrections on work submitted by the country's top comic book artists. It was a great learning experience as I had to make corrections in the styles of many different artists. I began to receive assignments from several editors and drew for Western, Humor, Detective, Romance and War Stories comics.

One top editor at the company wanted me to work for him exclusively. He was known as a hard taskmaster but I decided to take the challenge and gave up all my other assignments to work for him. He was tough indeed and things worked out for three years and just as I felt confident enough as an artist to buy our first home my boss suddenly decided my work was unsatisfactory. Lesson learned: don't put all your eggs in one basket.

My unemployment was short-lived as my experience and reputation led to many assignments with other publishers. Soon I became a regular contributor to a fledgling publication called MAD magazine. In the 40 years that followed, MAD has become a national and international showcase for my work. That exposure helped spawn a successful and rewarding career creating art for advertising, TV commercials, magazine covers and book illustrations.

One of the most rewarding aspects of my career are the hundreds of letters I receive from around the world from young people who hope to become artists. I also get the opportunity to lecture at colleges and other groups. I tell these students and young professional artists that if they have the desire they should make a committment and never abandon their dreams. This committment includes constant striving to enhance your talents - doing your best work every time out - being true to yourself - accepting the inevitable fact that you can't please everyone - and realizing that every setback can be a setup for a giant leap forward. If you do all that, surely success will follow.

I also stress in talks that for every 100 people competing for a position 25 will make halfhearted attempts to compete for the job and will soon fade; 25 may be marginally talented and achieve marginal results; 25 will reach the first plateau, and remain there. That leaves only the top 25 to compete with. Not bad odds for those who are truly committed to making their dreams come true.

I hope I've given your readers something to draw upon whether they dream of a career as an artist or any other wonderful field.

Sincerely,

Mort Drucker

"Right is right, even if everyone is against it, and wrong is wrong, even if everyone is for it."

William Penn

BARBARA EDEN

ACTRESS

...brought the beguiling "Jeannie" of the sitcom "I Dream Of Jeannie" to television for five delightful years. She continues to appear in motion pictures, television roles and theater.

From high school days in San Francisco, Barbara Eden had a goal to succeed in show business. By the age of 16, she was an accomplished singer. By 19 she felt she was ready for Hollywood where she was summarily rejected without even being given a chance to perform. Barbara was supported by an encouraging family who knew her talent and urged her to continue. She continued to seek her dream, and found her "big break" under a non-exclusive contract at a studio for a new TV series "How to Marry a Millionaire," which lasted two seasons.

Then the Hollywood offers began coming in, with Barbara being selected for roles in the films: "Voyage to the Bottom of the Sea," "The Wonderful World of the Brothers Grim," and "The Seven Faces of Dr. Lao." Barbara also excelled as a singer and starred in several highly successful tours of such musicals as "Woman of the Year" and "South Pacific."

Barbara continues to capture the hearts and imagination of her audience with her acting and singing ventures. Personally, I'll always remember her as the star of "I Dream of Jeannie." Growing up, that show was one of my favorites and is still popular to thousands today!

Barbara Eden

Andy Andrews
P.O. Box 2761
Gulf Shores, AL 36547

Dear Andy,

Like most people making the journey through life, I have had many ups and downs but luckily it all evened out to what I feel has been a very productive and happy life.

One experience that shaped my thinking and actions at the beginning of my career in Hollywood was eye opening for me and might be for others beginning in the acting field.

I had just moved from San Francisco to live with my aunt and uncle in San Marino in order to pursue my singing and acting career. I was a member of Actor's Equity and had appeared on stage since I was 16 years old but I had only one contact in Los Angeles. That contact was the head of casting at Warner Brothers Studios.

On the day of my appointment, my uncle drove me to the studios as I didn't know how to drive a car (very inconvenient in L.A.). After briefly meeting the casting agent, and before I could even read for him, he told me abruptly, "You're a pretty kid and probably from a nice family. Why you don't go back to your family and marry the boy next door?" He then picked up a picture of his daughter and pointed to her bosom area. He bellowed out, "This is what they want - big ____!"

It makes me laugh now to recall this incident but at the time I felt like a bucket of ice water had been tossed over my dreams. Needless to say, I went home and cried copious tears. At one point during my emotional storm, I had a moment of calm and clear thinking. I realized that:
  A)   He hadn't heard me sing
  B)   He hadn't asked me to read
  C)   In fact, he hadn't asked me anything about my experience
I concluded that though this had been a negative experience, it was a necessary one. Perhaps one day I would take what I learned from that incident to the stage or screen. So I dried my tears and decided that large mammories not withstanding, I would proceed as a character actress.

Four months later, I was once again on the Warner Brothers lot. This time I was on my way to an acting lesson with a coach from the talent department when I heard someone yell, "Hey, you!" I kept walking since the coach was giving me free lessons and I wasn't supposed to be on the lot. The yelling continued, "Hey, you - you in the yellow pants." Well, I couldn't ignore it any longer and I turned around to face the same man I'd had the disastrous interview with. My heart stopped. I was certain that he was going to kick me off the lot. He walked up to me and asked, "What is your name?" I told him. He then said in loud, enunciated tones, "We're going to test you!" Huh, so much for a well endowed bosom. The man never even remembered me.

I learned a lesson that day that I've carried with me throughout my professional and personal life - don't let anyone's subjective opinion of you or your ability block your way on your chosen path.

Best Regards,

Barbara Eden

Barbara Eden

*"There are no shortcuts to
any place worth going."*

Sarah Brown

WILLIAM CHILDS WESTMORELAND

GENERAL UNITED STATES ARMY RETIRED

...commanded US troops in Vietnam for over four years. In 1965, Time *featured him as "Man of the Year.*

I have occasionally wondered what it would be like to have my name forever recorded in the pages of American history. Upon my first consideration, such thoughts were very appealing to me. I pictured school aged kids fantasizing they were me because of some great, memorable deed I had done, or of memorials and high schools bearing my name in honor of my memory. I then considered the prospect of having future generations learn about me and weighing accomplishments of my life on the scales of freedom. These scales would, of course, then be counterweighted by what will later become public opinion, political correctness and popularity. It suddenly became a very frightening thought.

Certainly, the Vietnam war has become a prominent point in American history and a historical event our children will learn about for generations to come. As the commander of all US armed forces in Vietnam, General William C. Westmoreland's name will be recorded there, to be weighed against the lessons of time and the opinions of the history writers.

To be sure, the formidable opposition the General faced while in this position was incredible; not only on the fighting lines, but on the home front as well. It has taken 20 years since the cessation of US involvement in Vietnam for any display of national support to manifest itself in the honor of our military's valiant efforts and sacrifice on the battlefields to which they were called. A storm of perfection, the sounds of which may still reveal echoes of the once pealing thunder.

William Childs Westmoreland
General, United States Army, Retired
Box 1059
Charleston, South Carolina   29402

Dear Andy,

In between World War I and Vietnam many of us Americans saw action in the largest of all Wars - World War II - and one of our longest wars in Korea, which is not yet concluded since fighting was stopped by an armistice. Meanwhile, those soldiers of my vintage had thrown into their laps our military commitment to South Vietnam.

Wars, or military conflicts, are all different but all have similarities--people are killed and wounded by weapons manned by people. The numbers of casualties are more a function of time on the battlefield rather than weapons of destruction. Our battlefield foes - Germany, Japan, North Korea, and North Vietnam - were prepared for that contingency. The United States, as a democratic country, was not.

As a young officer my first assignment was with a military unit armed with weapons of Franco-Prussion War vintage drawn by teams of six horses. But, some 26 years later, I found myself fighting an unpopular war in Southeast Asia which few understood, and a war where our strategy was restrained by the fear that the Chinese would be drawn to the battlefield as in Korea.

It was my lot, and my privilege, to command those fine young Americans in that unique conflict where our national objective was ambigious and, thus, public support marginal.

Our national leadership - Our President - wished to turn the battlefield over to the South Vietnamese and plans were projected to do that, but such a strategy was subsequently over-taken by an act of Congress that made it unlawful to provide any further aid of any kind to the South Vietnamese government.

Every generation has its challenges, and the generation of Americans that carried the burdens of the 1960's and 70's had a uniquely heavy load. They did their best and have no apologies. They played a unique and major role in the making our World safe for democracy and America leader of nations.

Sincerely,

William C. Westmoreland

JEANNE WHITE

FOUNDER/RYAN WHITE FOUNDATION

...is on the board of the American Foundation for AIDS Research. Her son contracted AIDS from a tainted blood product. Ryan died Sunday, April 8, 1990.

Jeanne White lost her young son, Ryan, to AIDS in 1990 as a result of a blood transfusion he'd received 6 years previously. This was a storm in itself but was only compounded by the reactions of friends and people in general to her son's diagnosed condition. Though it was grounded in ignorance, the rejection Jeanne experienced for herself and her son still heaped sorrow upon sorrow. They actually had to move from their home and find a new place to live, as schools and the communities turned a cold shoulder to them. It was an experience which could either permanently embitter Jeanne's spirit, or bring to the surface her extraordinary qualities of patience and forgiveness.

Jeanne is now deeply involved with AIDS education and the battle for increased research. She is on the board of the American Foundation for AIDS research, has testified before congress and has worked with the publisher on her son's autobiography. She is the founder and president of "The Ryan White Foundation." The foundation's mission is to continue Ryan's legacy of education by increasing awareness of personal, family and community issues related to HIV/AIDS and teenagers.

Mr. Andy Andrews
P.O. Box 2761
Gulf Shores, AL 36547

Dear Andy:

When you asked me to write about my greatest disappointment I was honored that you asked me to contribute to your book but a little nervous about sharing the story of my disappointment with you.

When my son, Ryan, was diagnosed with AIDS in 1984, our entire world changed almost overnight. We were befriended by celebrities, shunned by Ryan's school and forced into the public eye by the media. Reactions ranged from total support to total rejection of Ryan and our family.

But my greatest disappointment came at the hands of the woman I considered my best friend. You see, we had been friends since grade school. We had played together, gone to school together, double-dated and shared all the things two best friends share over nearly thirty years. We were in each other's weddings. In fact, we wore the same bridesmaid dress!

Unfortunately, when my friend found out Ryan had AIDS she began to withdraw from us. Suddenly her children couldn't play with my children. She no longer wanted to visit me or go shopping with me or have lunch with me. At a time in my life when I needed a friend more than ever - she wasn't there for me.

At first I was hurt and I was angry. How could my best friend abandon me? Ryan was the biggest help to me in understanding my friend's reaction. When I got upset over the way people were treating us, Ryan would say, "They are just scared and they are trying to protect their kids like you're trying to protect me."

Now, five years after Ryan's death, my best friend and I are rebuilding our relationship. Am I bitter? No, of course not. I learned from Ryan that good people sometimes do bad things because they need education. That's why I started The Ryan White Foundation - to educate people, especially adolescents and teens, about HIV and AIDS. If we do our jobs, other families won't lose their friends because of ignorance and fear.

Sincerely,

Jeanne White

Jeanne White

WINK MARTINDALE

TELEVISION PERSONALITY

...has hosted 21 television game shows, including the highly successful "Tic-Tac-Dough."

Wink Martindale has been a television and radio personality for years. Wink has hosted more TV game shows than any other TV host; in history, 21 shows in all. These include "What's This Song," "Can You Top This," "Gambit," "High Rollers" and the highly successful "Tic-Tac-Dough."

Wink's work on radio and TV has spanned nearly 40 years. His insights to success and happiness are profound. I am reminded that even a person associated with light-hearted entertainment has seen his share of adversity. Wink has a knowledge and understanding of successful principles which he shares in his letter.

Wink Martindale's attitude and approach toward the adversity he has faced reveal once again that problems can be a springboard to success. He continues to head his own production company and is currently hosting four game shows on the Family Channel's game show block.

Andy Andrews
P. O. Box 2761
Gulf Shores, AL 36547

Dear Andy:

Thanks for the opportunity to be a part of your newest edition of *Storms of Perfection*. I admire what this series of books stand for, and I applaud you for bringing these far ranging stories to our attention.

"Didn't you used to be Wink Martindale?" Believe it or not, this is a question I have been asked more than once by a well-meaning television viewer. Another favorite is, "What would you eventually like to do?" They seem almost shocked when I reply that I am already *doing* what I want to do.

As any good game show contestant knows, the distance between Mars and Hollywood generally is measured in light years. However, it is this unlikely course that I have traveled. More than 38 years ago, fresh out of Memphis State University with a major in Speech and Drama and a minor in Journalism, my first TV assignment was as star of a local children's show, "Wink Martindale of the Mars Patrol", a combination of several kids, Bosco and milk and old Flash Gordon films.

Two years later I came back down to Earth, hosting a teen dance program, "Top Ten Dance Party".......the Dick Clark of Memphis. After blasting off to Mars with adolescent astronauts and dancing the peppermint twist with teenagers, I left the security of "home" for the bright lights of "la la land", Los Angeles. It was here that I discovered America's infatuation with game shows, and that *real people* are, in my view, much more exciting than a group of dramatic characters in a script. And on the up side, over the years I've been hugged and kissed more times than your average prime time hunk! Plus I'm almost as recognizable as the Vice-President of the United States. "What would I *eventually* like to do?" Are you kidding?

1330 South Glendale Avenue • Glendale, CA 91205 • Tel (818)502-5550 • Fax (818)502-5554

So the greater part of my life has been a game. With the same ingredients necessary for a successful game show.......compelling, interesting, suspenseful, competitive, and fun. In fact, I am told that after hosting "Trivial Pursuit" and three other shows on The Family Channel during 1993-94, I hold the record for hosting the *most* television game shows, 21. Yet it hasn't all been "fun and games". Unlike Bob Barker's 23 year statement, the "Price" wasn't always "Right!" My 30 years of work to insure a place in television yore, saw my first marriage of 18 years end in divorce and my son battle drug addiction from age 12 to the present. And losses in unfortunate restaurant, real estate and business partnerships created a loss of well over a million dollars.

But all-in-all, I was lucky; I wanted a career in radio [and later television]. And I set out at an early age to make that commitment, without procrastinating. I am reminded of a poem written by 14 year old Jason Lehman, a talented young poet beyond his years:

PRESENT TENSE

It was Spring,
But it was summer I wanted, The warm days,
And the great outdoors.
It was summer,
But it was fall I wanted, The colorful leaves,
And the cool, dry air.
It was fall,
But it was winter I wanted, The beautiful snow,
And the joy of the holiday season.
It was winter,
But it was spring I wanted, The warmth,
And the blossoming of nature.
I was a child,
But it was adulthood I wanted, The freedom,
And the respect.
I was 20,
But it was 30 I wanted, To be mature,
And sophisticated.
I was middle-aged,
But it was 20 I wanted, The youth,
And the free spirit.
I was retired,
But it was middle-age I wanted,
The presence of mind,
Without limitations.

My life was over.
But I never got what I wanted.

What a simple message really. Make up your mind. Set your goal, or goals, and go for them! Don't procrastinate. Thankfully, God sent me that message at a young age. Everything else being equal, the guy who has the most genuine enthusiasm for his work will do the best job. And don't pay much attention to a guy's chronological age. Some people are 60 going on 40 and some are 20 going on 70. A mature person is a person of any age who has learned from his experiences. A young person is a person of any age who is driven to be successful.

In my view, any success I have enjoyed came entirely from within, and with strong spiritual values. Successful people achieve success because of their performance. They do more than the average person, they do it better than the average person, and the do _their best_, almost all the time. Roosevelt had infantile paralysis. It didn't keep him down. Nothing could. Only death. He worked with what was left him: his head, his humor, his heart. Helen Keller: deaf, blind. She pursued life. She had a vision; she pursued it.

The following poem has meant a great deal to me because, if there is such a thing as the _definition_ of success, it is in these few lines:

> To laugh often and much:
> To win the respect of intelligent people
> and the affection of children;
> To earn the appreciation of honest critics
> and endure the betrayal of false friends;
> To appreciate beauty;
> To find the best in others;
> To leave the world a bit better whether by
> a healthy child, a redeemed social condition
> or a job well done;
> To know even one other life has breathed easier
> because you lived;
> This is to have succeeded.
>
> **Anonymous**

Best personal regards,

Wink Martindale

BOB REESE

BUSINESSMAN

...is the 43-year-old Vice President of Flowdata, Inc. Bob has recently been featured in US News and World Reports.

Bob Reese grew up in the Dallas area and graduated from college in St. Louis. Almost immediately, Bob began his career as an assistant manager with INOTEK TECHNOLOGIES. In 1991, after several years as the company's CEO and majority owner, he sold the company. During the 20 year period that Bob worked with INOTEK, he was responsible for leading it from a small company with only three employees to a company with annual sales of 30 million dollars and 150 employees.

Bob now lives with Connie, his wife of 18 years, and their eight children, ranging in age from 2 to 17. Bob has been featured in *US News and World Report* and is an active participant in Republican Party politics.

Bob Reese
Route 4 Box 376
Canton, Texas 75103

Andy Andrews
P.O. Box 2761
Gulf Shores, Alabama 36547

Dear Andy,

It was great to receive your request for a letter! I feel that if anyone can benefit in some small way from what I have learned in my business and personal life, writing this will be time well spent.

I believe my "moment of truth" came in June of 1977. I was General manager of our family business at that time. A group of well meaning but unhappy employees approached me and shared their feelings about my management style. They were not getting the kind of leadership they needed from me to do the job I required of them. True self assessment is never particularly easy. What bothered me most was the feeling that I had let the team members down.

From that point forward I began to redefine the way I thought of others. I began to adjust my management style to a complete _team_ effort. I literally began to live the business gospel of "I" as being nobody and "We" as a team being able to accomplish anything. As a Christian, I began to shift my philosophy of management to a more Biblically based management style. I bolstered this change in my thinking with a commitment to three things: **Patience, Persistence, and Prayer.** As I prayed continually for wisdom and guidance to make the right decisions for the team, I became more patient with people and yet could apply appropriate persistence to achieve certain goals and objectives .

Then, moving into the early '80s we were challenged once again by a number of things. The economy took a downturn which hurt business in general. We experienced an explosion in our facility. These and several other business trials seemed to happen one after another. Had we not adjusted the way we were relating as a business team, these occurrences might have spelled the end of the company. Instead, we made it through and during the mid to late '80s we grew substantially. In 1989 I was able to successfully sell this business to a public company.

I learned that surrounding yourself with strong, good people allows you to be stronger yourself. Using the Bible as a basis for my own life has given me strengths and successes to share with others. We can only accomplish the great things we set out to accomplish if we work together as a team. This concept is true in business or politics or sports or family life.

Looking back, Andy, if those unhappy employees hadn't had the guts to tell me how they were feeling back in 1977, who knows where we would be today. I certainly wouldn't be preparing to take the principles I have learned into the Texas State Senate race!

Patience, Persistence and Prayer.

Bob Reese

JOAN KENLEY

SPEAKING VOICE EXPERT

Photo by Russ Fischella, S.F.

...is a renowned speaking voice expert, psychologist and author, providing her lecture, seminar and consulting services nationally and internationally.

Joan Kenley is the most listened to public speaker in America. I believe it would be safe to say that everyone of us has been part of Joan Kenley's audience many times - most of us on a daily basis. She certainly encompasses a broader audience than any other public speaker.

Joan is known world-wide for her friendly voice on such digitized services as Pacific Bell's Message Center, Northern Telecom's Meridian Mail, Nynex directory assistance, and American Personal Communications wireless products. Her voice is heard in businesses, homes, hotels, voice fax mail, wireless voice mail, elevators, clocks and talking cash registers.

Joan is the author of *Voice Power*, a book which details her Body Voice Method for improving the sound of one's voice. She is also a psychologist, who lives in the California San Francisco Bay area. After the 1989 San Francisco earthquake, Joan counseled hundreds over a local radio station to assist them in handling their fears and anxieties. Joan is also a former actress who has worked in the past with such greats as Ethel Merman and Jackie Gleason.

Joan has enjoyed success in a broad spectrum of ventures; her rise to success did not come of mere good fortune but was born out of the fears and insecurities of a little girl, as her letter reflects.

Joan Kenley signature

Joan Kenley, Ph.D.
1 800 820 2010

Dear Andy,

When I was nine years old and happily naive, a mother of one of my pal's yelled meanly at me in front of my friends—"I heard you the first time. Sit down and shut up!"—because I had repeated to her more than once that my mother was going to arrive late. She made me sit facing the room for an hour while the others played. My face burned, my heart pounded, and my body shook.

After that incident, I developed a hidden introversion. I tried to adopt a female version of my physician-father's voice, hoping to sound secure by emulating my dad's assuring confidence. I wanted my voice to reflect the heroine of my young ambitions. Yet, inside, I was very sensitive and cautious. I tried to escape disapproval by constantly checking for signals from others.

My father died suddenly of a stroke. I was only 14. Trying to be strong for my mother, I developed a strange conflict. Most of the time, I could project a brave voice to the world, but whenever I felt self-doubting or vulnerable —my mother's soft, timid voice would emerge. I found myself caught in a vocal tug-of-war.

During extreme pressure, it would be hard to breathe and my throat would tighten as if I were strangling. I was never sure what sound I would present from one day to the next. Yet, I *knew* in the future my voice would be heard by many—I just didn't know how.

After my college years at Denison University in Ohio, I soon realized I needed to train myself to overcome my midwest accent—changing words like "jist" and "warsh" and "git" to their true pronunciation. Yet throughout my twenties—when I was both an actress and corporate businesswoman in New York City—I still worked desperately to find my *real* vocal sound—one that reflected clarity, heart and substance.

I began to experiment with techniques that combined breathing and body awareness, along with tension and emotional release. Eventually, I developed a series of vocal warm-ups that were always reliable. I became known for my voice, recording countless radio and television commercials.

Later, I acquired a Ph.D. in body/mind psychology to enhance my understanding. Over the years, my personal vocal work-out evolved into my BodyVoice Method for improving the sound of the speaking voice—not just for myself, but others as well. In 1989, my book VOICE POWER (Henry Holt & Co.) was published. I am proud to say it has helped more people than I could have imagined.

Fifteen years ago, out of the blue, I was offered an opportunity to record some of the first digital voice products—the talking cash register in grocery stores, elevators and clocks. These experiences led to major contracts to record large voice mail systems for homes and businesses, hotel guest messaging, wireless voice answering services and voice fax mail. I've become the most frequently heard voice in America. What a rewarding irony to find my voice everywhere—when in my early years my speaking voice was such a source of anguish!

Very best regards,

Joan Kenley, Ph.D.

*"The split in you is clear...
there is a part of you that
knows what it should do and
a part that does what it feels
like doing."*

John Cantwell Kiley

RANDALL ARTHUR

MINISTER/AUTHOR

...is the author of two Christian fiction novels. Despite its controversial tone, Wisdom Hunter *is one of the most consistently recommended Christian novels on the market today.*

Randall Arthur is noted for his best selling Christian fiction novel, *Wisdom Hunter.* He is a pastor and author who has brought controversy in some circles of Christianity, while using part of his own life's story as a basis for the novel. The first novel resulted in Randall's termination from his pastoral position, while the book was being bought and read by thousands in the general Christian community.

Randall Arthur has written a second novel, *Jordan's Crossing*, which has met with as much success as his first. He is currently working on a third novel of Christian fiction with expectations of continued fantastic response from readers everywhere.

Randall Arthur has suffered rejection because of his faith and because of his books. As he points out in his letter, however, "pain does not have to be wasted." It can be used as a tool to make us better.

RANDALL ARTHUR

Andy Andrews
P.O. Box 2761
Gulf Shores, Alabama 36547

Dear Andy,

Thanks for helping create *laughter* in the world with your special humor.

And thanks equally for helping spread *hope* and *encouragement* through your "Storms Of Perfection" volumes.

I'm honored to contribute to this latest edition. I trust that my letter, combined with all the others, will help readers in the midst of life's struggles realize <u>it's always too early to give up</u>.

I became a Christian at the age of thirteen. I was nurtured for the next ten years by well-meaning saints who convinced me that my relationship with God would be ruined if I attended a movie, grew a beard, listened to a Karen Carpenter song (or any "pop" music), read from a Bible translation other than the King James Version, or committed any other *"indecent"* act that their religious tradition classified as sin.

At the age of 23 I moved with my 19 year old bride to Oslo, Norway, where I became a pastor of a multinational church. I was sponsored by a large American mission organization and sixty stateside churches. I zealously preached the legalistic type of Christianity I had been taught, believing that my denomination had a monopoly on truth and had developed Christianity to its maximum potential. I believed that anyone who was different from me was wrong, ignorant, blind, and in jeopardy of damnation.

Fortunately, the people in my Oslo congregation - engineers, doctors, teachers, embassy personnel, NATO officers, etc. - were not intimidated by my self-righteous and authoritarian attitude. They constantly challenged me to examine what I was preaching. "You're not teaching Christianity," they would tell me, "you're teaching your Bible-belt traditions in the name of God and imprisoning people by them." Over a two to three year period they eventually help me see that the issues which I considered to be the heart of true spirituality were not

Biblical at all, but were simply denominational prejudices, the personal convictions of idolized leaders, and the preferences of my native culture - *just empty baggage.*

I finally realized that I had spent over ten years of my life misrepresenting Christianity. At that point I began a swing from the far right that thrust me into a seven year pilgrimage of trying to restructure my life. This pilgrimage - laden with confusion, disillusionment, anger, bitterness, frustration, burn out, loss of heart, and finally apathy - nearly destroyed my marriage, my ministry, and even left me death wishing.

During this pilgrimage I learned some important lessons and insights about the short and long-term effects of spiritual abuse that I felt my legalistic peers desperately needed to hear. I knew, however, that these people would never listen to me face to face. So, I decided to write a novel and wrap these insights into an adventurous real-life drama that hopefully they would listen to.

As it happened, WISDOM HUNTER, my first novel was born. It is a novel that was born out of much pain, many tears, and a therapeutic need to put into writing the things I was feeling, thinking, and learning. It is a novel that attempts to illustrate the destructiveness of religious legalism.

I spent three years writing the book in my spare time. I spent another year sending copies of the completed manuscript to various publishing houses in the States. The manuscript was continually rejected for publication until it was reviewed by Questar Publishers in Oregon. When Questar offered to publish the book nationwide I gratefully signed the contract. Upon the book's release a few months later, WISDOM HUNTER became an immediate bestseller in Christian bookstores throughout America. It was nominated by 'Christianity Today' for the Book-Of-The-Year award for Christian fiction.

At the same time, however, the book proved to be too controversial for my denomination. Upon reading WISDOM HUNTER, the president of the mission agency with which I had served for seventeen years fired me literally overnight. Within a matter of weeks nearly all of my sponsoring churches reacted with equal offense, quickly severing their relationship with me. Consequently, I lost nearly my entire network of lifelong constituents and over 65% of my income. I was 38 years old.

Starting over in life was not easy, but I was left without any other viable options. As difficult as it was, however, the new beginning proved to be a major stepping stone. Not only did I find a new and healthier direction as a pastor, but I was also launched into a secondary career as a successful novelist. I am now working on my third novel, with the first two currently being translated into several foreign languages. The transition also brought me into contact with a whole new network of friends, the most wonderful and understanding friends I have ever known. My life, ministry, and marriage have never been more fruitful, peaceful, and joyful than they are at the present.

I have learned that pain does not have to be wasted. If we spend time reviewing our pain and learning from it rather than simply regretting it, we will discover that pain, like no other source, can successfully supply our hearts and minds with invaluable wisdom, understanding, knowledge, and insight.

Would I face the pain, upheaval, and rejection all over again to learn what I now know? The answer is an unequivocal YES!

Sincerely,

Randall Arthur

Randall Arthur
Pastor/Author

TOMMY HILFIGER

CLOTHING DESIGNER

...presiding over one of the largest and most successful men's sportswear companies in the USA, Tommy is widely acclaimed as the leading American menswear designer of the 1990's.

You may have heard it said, "The clothes make the man." The fact of the matter, according to Tommy Hilfiger, is that one's response to the difficult situations in life is what really makes the man. We will all suffer adversity from time to time, but it is Tommy's philosophy that one can make a good thing come from a bad experience.

Tommy Hilfiger is at the helm of one of the largest and most successful men's sportswear companies in America. He came from a large family for which he found himself providing at an age when most other boys could be found playing baseball. A true example of the American dream, Tommy began his journey into the business world with $150, twenty pairs of jeans and one good idea.

It was not easy to overcome the odds against him. He felt compelled to stretch himself out of his comfort zone and reach for something greater than most (perhaps even Tommy) had ever expected him to achieve. Tommy credits his notoriety and good fortune to his adaptability and positive approach to handling difficult times. He emphasizes that anyone can create their own success if they will make the resolute choice to take a negative situation and turn it into a positive one, and that a positive, uplifting attitude is the key that unlocks one's possibility to do so.

Andy Andrews
Lightning Crown Publishers
POB 17321
Nashville, TN 37217

Dear Andy:

I'm not sure how you selected me to contribute to your book, *Storms of Perfection III*. However, I am most honored to share my perspective.

I started working when I was eleven years old and I opened my first business when I was 18 years old. My pursuit grew into a successful business within ten years.

The next ten years became another interesting challenge. I entered into a field I knew little about but had a passion for. I wanted to become a fashion designer without going through the normal procedure of going to fashion school. I struggled with odd jobs in the industry trying to learn as much as possible. Today I preside over one of the largest menswear companies in America. I believe the insight I can provide is meaningful because it has to do with taking a negative and turning it into a positive.

When I was growing up, I was part of a large family of nine children. I had to provide for myself as well as my siblings. Many people may have found this to be a very negative situation. I took it as a great opportunity to learn that honest work can be rewarding and challenging. Today my work is just that, both challenging and rewarding.

Thank you for this opportunity to re-look at the amazing journey I am on, and to appreciate again how I got here. I believe that if one wants to succeed, the key is to think positively as well as being honest, and passionate about what you do.

Sincerely,

Tommy Hilfiger

Tommy Hilfiger U.S.A., Inc.
25 West 39th Street   New York, NY 10018
(212) 840-8888   Fax (212) 302-8718

DANIEL "RUDY" RUETTIGER

MOTIVATIONAL SPEAKER

...inspired the Tri-Star major motion picture "Rudy." Rudy travels internationally as a top motivational and inspirational speaker.

Rudy's story plays out like a classic fairy tale, with the hero emerging victorious over innumerable and insurmountable obstacles. But a fairy tale is just that, a fictional story created out of our hopes that something spectacular could really happen. When the matter is reality, it is all the more an inspiring testament to the human spirit.

Rudy played for the Notre Dame University's fighting Irish football team for 27 seconds of the last home game of his senior year. It was his last chance to play in a game. Rudy's dedication to his dream and his endurance of continual struggles inspired his team mates to carry him off the field at the end of that game, with the entire stadium chanting RU-DY! RU-DY! Rudy is the only Notre Dame player since 1975 to be carried off the field in victory.

Rudy's story of overcoming his life's challenges to ultimately achieve his dream is the subject of a feature film "Rudy," from Tri-Star pictures, and a book entitled *Rudy's Rules*. Today, Rudy is a highly sought-after motivational speaker. His "dream big" and "never quit" attitude inspires entrepreneurs, CEOs, sales people, college and professional sports teams, as well as students around the country.

Rudy

"Never Give Up On Your Dreams"

Andy Andrews
P.O. Box 2761
Gulf Shores, Alabama 36547

Dear Andy,

It's a real privilege to contribute to your effort. As you know, the circumstances surrounding me playing football for the University of Notre Dame have become my life testimony to never giving up on your dreams. What many people don't realize is there are many, many little defeats and little victories along the way that actually make up the final success.

For example, we all have dreams as children which we literally "play out" with our friends and brothers and sisters. With me those dreams revolved around Notre Dame football. But to even get into that University your grades have to be really top notch. My teachers told my parents that I was a problem child and not very bright. My parents of course believed what the trained educators told them and reflected it back to me. I also believed for a time that I was stupid. So, when I voiced my dream of one day playing Notre Dame football, my family and friends thought they were protecting me by trying to get me to focus in a less ambitious direction. They didn't want me to get hurt. But what happens through this process, if you hold onto your dream, is you begin to get angry. You get mad at the situation and the people giving you the wrong information. Then you learn to focus that anger in the areas that will prove the information wrong. In my case I found out later that I had a learning disorder. I wasn't stupid at all!

I worked through it and when the time came I applied to Notre Dame. I was rejected. In fact that first rejection was the worst of all. I was so eager to reach my ultimate dream, Notre Dame football, that I became impatient. I almost missed understanding the necessary priority of accomplishing what I wanted. But, through holding onto my dream, I learned patience. I applied every semester and was rejected every semester. I knew I had to convince them that I was serious. I didn't want them to take me lightly. So I kept applying. Finally, I was accepted. It was the last possible semester I could have been accepted and still played football.

Was that step one? Or was it step 200? Did it begin with my brothers and me in the backyard? Or with the teachers telling my parents I was stupid? I don't know. I do know that it was the direct result of having - and holding - a dream. Of course I did go on to play football for Notre Dame, then made the movie, RUDY, which in many ways was even more challenging than playing Notre Dame football! But the process in playing football or making the movie or having a book published or reaching any dream is the same. And it will work for Rudy or anyone. Focus on your ultimate dream then understand the priority of steps to get it. Then never - ever - ever let it go.

1583 N. Oakhill • South Bend, IN 46637 • Phone/Fax (219) 277-1241

I'm often asked "What was your proudest moment, Rudy?" I think people are expecting a story from Notre Dame. But I remember the day my little league coach took the team to a big league game. He caught a foul ball and asked "Who wants it?" Of course everybody wanted it. So he said that after the game we'd stop off at the little league field and have the team line up behind home plate. Then he'd hit it into the outfield and whoever got it first could have it. I don't remember the rest of the game after that. I sat and replayed a vision of me outrunning everyone and getting the ball over and over in my mind. And, when the time came, I got the ball. That is still a big deal to me.

So, Andy, I guess the question is "Who wants it?" The process works for anyone who wants anything bad enough to focus and learn until they get it!

Keep fighting the good fight!

Dream Big
Never Quit!

Daniel "Rudy" Ruettiger

"I count him braver who overcomes his desires than him who conquers his enemies; for the hardest victory is the victory over self."

Aristotle

SCOTT DeGARMO

BUSINESSMAN

...is Editor in Chief and Publisher of SUCCESS *Magazine.* SUCCESS *is the country's fastest growing business magazine.*

Scott DeGarmo became editor-in-chief, of *SUCCESS* Magazine in 1984, and added the title of Publisher in 1990, making him one of the few editor/publishers in the consumer magazine field.

Upon assuming the role of editor-in-chief, DeGarmo quickly turned *SUCCESS* into the country's fastest growing business magazine. It reaches a total of more than 1.25 million readers each month and, on the newsstand, *SUCCESS* outsells all business magazines.

DeGarmo subtitled *SUCCESS* "The Magazine for Today's Entrepreneurial Mind," noting that it is aimed at business owners, and entrepreneurially minded business people.

Scott is known for spending a certain portion of every day talking on the phone, or in person, with his readers and encourages his editors to do the same.

I have been a subscriber of *SUCCESS* for years and am one of the many people who have been influenced by Scott and his work. I am grateful for the attitude of persistence he displayed early in his career. The decisions he made then are still at work today!

SCOTT DeGARMO
EDITOR IN CHIEF & PUBLISHER (212) 551-9414

Andy Andrews
P.O. Box 2761
Gulf Shores, Alabama 36547

Dear Andy,

When I sat down to write this letter I had a difficult time recalling exactly what "my story" was. As I looked back I was able to recall my share of sweating, struggling, and striving in my progression to my current position as Editor of *Success*, but in retrospect, I felt grateful for every moment of trial and hardship. While they often seemed unbearable at the time, their memory makes the present that much sweeter.

I remembered my early days of research concerning *Success* and its original founder/ editor Orison Swett Marden, my hero. I found his middle name, pronounced "sweat" (as in perspiration) of some interest! It seems Mr. Marden was orphaned early in life. As a youngster he stumbled across a fabulous 19th century self-help book (entitled *Self-Help*) and stayed up all night reading it. The next day Marden ran away from his foster home determined to get a quality education and rise to his potential. Though not a very good student at first, he later received degrees from Harvard Medical School and Boston Law School *simultaneously.* He went on to become a successful entrepreneur in several ventures, and in his middle age, (over 100 years ago) decided to create a publication that was designed to highlight the successes of the great entrepreneurs of the day. He wanted to show the "strugglers and strivers of the world" that they could do what Ford, Carnegie and Rockefeller had done by showing them examples of the *process of success*.   He wanted to shorten the distance between points A and B where business success was concerned. His vision was powerfully optimistic and magnanimous.

I found this story incredibly inspiring. I recalled how I, as a young editor for the *Philadelphia Inquirer,* had a dream of creating a science magazine. I mocked-up some dummies of my idea and literally spent what little money I had on trains

230 PARK AVENUE, 7TH FLOOR • NEW YORK, NY 10169 • FAX (212) 599-0783

and hotels going to New York City in search of a publisher. While money was in short supply in those days there was no shortage of "friends" who told me "that's not how magazines are started... they're started by big companies... quit wasting your time and money." All I knew then was that I had to deep trying. How else would I know if my idea would work? I refused to hear the nay-sayers.

Finally, I received a call from Hearst Magazines. Someone there heard that I had been knocking on doors wanting to establish a science magazine. It so happened they owned a science title that they wanted to resurrect and wondered if I would discuss it with them. Opportunity met opportunity, a match was made and a science magazine was created. Who said that's not the way magazines are started?

This experience actually prepared me for my future with *Success*. I noticed that no matter how strongly or passionately a scientist believed in a theory, if it was not correct or it went against already established laws of nature it simply would not work. However, in the business world, if an entrepreneur believed in an idea strongly enough, I witnessed case after case of belief overcoming all odds to create success. This was certainly true in my own experience, and was so exciting that it ultimately led to my research into the Success Magazine of Orison Marden.

You see, Andy, as I made my way through obstacles to become the editor of a magazine, I learned that there were indeed ways to shorten the distance between points A and B. Perhaps the most important way was to *believe*. I determined then to share what I had found with today's entrepreneurs much like Orison Marden did over 100 years ago. *Success* Magazine was reborn. I see it as a fusion or marriage of ideas: between the logical processes of achievement on one hand, and Marden's belief in the unlimited potential of the individual, on the other. I believe that we are living in an age of the greatest opportunity humankind has ever known. To be a part of spreading this belief fills every moment of my life with challenge, passion, and excitement.

Believe,

Scott DeGarmo

"I hear and I forget.
I see and I remember.
I do and I understand."

Chinese Proverb

NORMAN D. VAUGHAN

MOUNTAIN CLIMBER/ DOG SLED RACER

...at the age of 72 he ran the 1200 mile Iditarod Sled Dog Race, Alaska's longest, most grueling dog race. Mount Vaughan, a mountain in the Antarctic, was named in his honor.

How often we hear children say, "When I grow up, I want to be an astronaut or a sailor or a pilot or an explorer of some sort." I believe at sometime or other, all of us have fantasized about being the first to break new ground - to risk the vast new wilderness and tread where only true adventurers dare to go. For most of us it remains just a fantasy. For Colonel Norman Vaughan it was (and still is) his life's quest.

I was amazed to learn of how Colonel Vaughan had subjected himself to an unpaid year of relentless training and rigorous preparations in order to win his reward of exposing himself to the grueling, unforgiving climate and demands of the last great continent, Antarctica. It was all for the noble sake of adventure that he met the challenges to even be accepted on Admiral Byrd's famed expedition; where the real life-challenging situations would manifest themselves. His experience of driving dog teams through the expansive wilderness of the seventh continent would stay with him for the rest of his life.

This was but the first of Colonel Vaughan's great adventures. Throughout his life, Colonel Vaughan has pursued his dreams. He has in fact suffered failure from time to time, as anyone will who is resolved to live life to its fullest. But those failures became stepping stones on a road map to greatness.

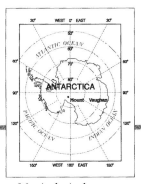

Mount Vaughan Antarctic Expedition

NORMAN D. VAUGHAN   4141 "B" STREET, SUITE 406   ANCHORAGE, AK 99503
TEL. 907-561-7344   FAX 907-562-0753

Mr. Andy Andrews
P. O. Box 2761
Gulf Shores, Alabama 36547

Dear Andy,

I have had so many failures in my 89 years of active life that I do not know where to begin.

Whether Harvard won the Yale game or not seemed overwhelmingly important. My vision had been on a prep school level. Now it was every story of football and whether or not I could make the freshman team. Suddenly as quick as I could read five words my whole life changed. The evening paper was tossed through the door. I read the banner headlines: "Byrd to the South Pole." I put the paper flat on the dining room table for my four roommates to see, "I've got to go." They thought I was just hot air and it was quite impossible.

But on the very next morning after dreaming all night about driving dogs across the Antarctic Ice Shelf just as Amundsen, Scott, Mawson, and Shackleton had done, I was at Commader Richard E. Byrd's home in Boston ready to sign on. I went up to the steps to the front door ready to have Commander Byrd accept my "signing-on." Instead a buxom maid who came to the door put her arms akimbo and with real authority said, "Nobody gets by me without an appointment!" After dreaming all night, I was stopped dead in my tracks, instantly shattered. I had to find another way. I thought of W. A. McDonald, the journalist. He could see Byrd for me.

I persisted in finding McDonald and gave him the following proposition to relay to Byrd: I was a dog driver, I knew the cold of Labrador, and I would leave Harvard College to go to New Hampshire to assemble and train his 100 dogs. And I would do all of this for no pay. I had winter clothes but no money to eat. I could sleep in any barn. I had a good sleeping bag. And Byrd would not have to accept or reject me until a year had passed when he was to leave Boston. My provisional plan was accepted.

I worked at a local inn so that I could have the food that was left on people's plates for my dinner and next day's breakfast and lunch. This was the only pay the innkeeper would give me. I slept in an open gazebo. And I trained hard readying for the expedition. I had gambled through persistence and 11 month later it paid off when Byrd took me on the expedition

Persistence and never taking "No" for an answer have shaped my life. I have always taken advantage of every opportunity that has come my way, forging a place for myself when others only see a closed door. This attitude took me to the 1932 Olympics the only time dog driving was an event, to the Battle of the Bulge with dog teams to rescue wounded soldiers, to Greenland to spearhead the rescue of 25 downed pilots by dog team, and then to the rescue of the P-38 planes themselves fifty years later under 264' of ice in the Greenland ice sheet.

I have gone through 3 failed marriages and with only $100 in my pocket, moved to Alaska. With no job and no money I shoveled sidewalks to earn meals at local restaurants. Later I found a job as a janitor cleaning commodes at the local university. From a life of luxury growing up, I had hit bottom. But I didn't despair. Instead of cleaning with one mop, I took pride in cleaning with two and having floors so clean that I literally ate breakfast off them to prove their cleanliness to my doubting boss. Ultimately I went on to become the stage manager for the theater.

Then at the age of 72 I ran the 1200 mile Iditarod Sled Dog Race, Alaska's longest, most grueling dog race. I have always been the oldest and slowest, but that never stopped me and I have raced in it 13 races.

My biggest dream has always been to return to the Antarctic to retrace our original route on the ice shelf and to climb a mountain that Admiral Byrd named for me: Mount Vaughan, 10,302' high. Finally, in 1993 that dream was about to come true after 2 years of overcoming all sorts of financial and political obstacles. Who wants to sponsor an 87 year old man to go down to the Antarctic and do what?! In November of '93 our first of 6 flights of a chartered DC6 took off for the ice from Punta Arenas, Chile with our 20 dogs and 3 team members on board. It was Thanksgiving Day. Appropriate. But the next morning we woke to the horrid news that the plane had crashed. No one or dog had died. Only our veterinarian was badly injured. And our $1,000,000 expedition was going no where.

When everyone would have quit, I couldn't. Absolutely crushed, I found another way to go down. But then we had 2 weeks of bad weather and couldn't move. Now I had to raise another $150,000 to return the following year. We did: my wife, myself, and 2 guides made it to the summit, December 16, 1995, three days before my 89th birthday.

My motto: "Dream big and dare to fail." It has served me well throughout life.

Sincerely,

Norman D. Vaughan

*"You make up your mind
before you start, that
sacrifice is part of the
package."*

Richard M. DeVos

BARBARA JOHNSON

AUTHOR

...is a popular humorist and conference speaker with a national following. Through her best-selling books, she has helped scores of hurting people.

Barbara Johnson is a humorist and a much sought after conference speaker. She is the founder of Spatula Ministries, a non-profit organization designed to "Peel parents off the ceiling with a spatula of love and begin them on the road of recovery." She is an author, who has written such books as *Where Does A Mother Go To Resign?*, *Stick a Geranium in Your Hat And Be Happy*, *Fresh Elastic For Stretched Out Moms* and *Splashes Of Joy In The Cesspools Of Life*.

Thousands of people cherish Barbara Johnson and her comforting, uplifting humor-filled wisdom as a heaven sent gift of love and laughter. Her wisdom is rooted in family tragedies of her own which have taught her that pain in life is an event, but misery is optional. Barbara recommends, as one of her book titles states, to "Pack up your gloomies in a great big box, then sit on the lid and laugh."

Barbara has given many people the will to laugh again, in spite of their personal tragedies. She insists that laughing in the face of adversity is not a form of denial, but a proven tool for managing stress, coping with pain and maintaining hope.

Barbara Johnson
Director

"To bind up the
brokenhearted"
Is. 61:1

Spatula Ministries
Providing restoration to the family

Box 444, La Habra, CA 90631 (310) 691-7369

Dear Andy:

What a delight to be asked to contribute a letter for your
new material! Your previous books have been such an inspiration
and I know the subsequent ones will do the same.

Because ours is a ministry of encouragement, and my own books deal
with that (the word encourage means to "fill the heart") I had to
think a while about when a rejection situation caused me real
concern. I didn't write a word until I was fifty years old,
which proves that even folks living between estrogen and death can
be productive, right? Since then I have seven books out plus
several mini-books and over a million of them are in print and
circulation now, including foreign languages and large print.
Three of them have been on the best-selling list at the same time
so indeed, it is a miracle how God has used these books.

Taking you back to when I began writing, a friend sent a tape of
my story including some newsletters and a small manuscript for
what I was intending to put in a book. This was directed to a
large Christian publishing company for their opinion. Eagerly I
sat by the mailbox waiting for their response. Finally, the tape,
newsletters, manuscript and a note came back to me.. with it
was a terse note of explanation: We are not interested in anything
you have to submit to us. Your appeal would be far too limited
for our use."

WOW! I knew I was inexperienced and a real beginning at writing,
but this was a low blow.. and from an outstanding Christian publisher
that I had admired.

Yet I knew that the Lord had promised me that if I would be His
conduit of love flowing to others, He would propel my efforts..
so I continued writing, only with more deliberation, more determination in my decision to inspire others by my own experiences.

Rejction CAN be a propellant to perservere.. to grasp even more
firmly.. to hang on no matter what... so eventually even rejection
can prove to be a blessing. It surely was to ME!

Joyfully,

Barb Johnson
Director SPATULA MINISTRIES

PAUL RODRIGUEZ

COMEDIAN/ACTOR

...is a comedian, actor, director and producer. One will recognize him from his roles in such films as "D.C. Cab," "Born in East L.A." and "Made in America."

Paul Rodriguez was born in Culican, Mexico, and relocated to East Los Angeles as a young boy. In 1977, after a stint in the Air Force, he entered Long Beach City College on the G.I. Bill. He obtained an Associate Arts degree, then went to California State, intent on becoming an attorney. During a theater course, he worked behind the scenes an a production of "The Glass Menagerie." Paul's comic wise cracks at the expense of the school's multi-racial cast prompted the acting teacher to take him to the Comedy Store in Los Angeles.

It was there where I first saw Paul. His attitude of light-heartedness was contagious from the beginning. Soon, he was opening major concerts and performing at colleges and comedy clubs all over the nation.

What allowed Paul to become successful? He explains, "My single most important quality is perseverance. Someone once asked me what part of 'NO' I didn't understand, and I said, 'Just the N and the O.'" All the people I admire were self-made. I believe that everyone makes their own fortune."

Pαul
RODRIGUEZ
PRODUCTIONS INC.

9538 Brighton Way • Suite 203
Beverly Hills • CA • 90210

Andy Andrews
P.O. Box 2761
Gulf Shores, Alabama 36547

Dear Andy,

It was great to hear you were considering a letter from me for your new book. You made the statement that it was surprising how many things I was into these days. Movies, writing, my comedy career, television acting and producing. If life has taught me anything up to this point it is not to rely on any one thing. Luck has no address, and it isn't a lady. I could sit around waiting for Spielberg to call and starve to death. No, success is something you *make* happen. Success is a daily positive thing, not a finish line you're running for. Success is also the next-door-neighbor of failure. Because you can learn how to do whatever you're trying to do by failing at it some. In my world there are no failures. There are people who keep trying until they succeed and people who quit. The only way not to succeed is to quit. And the thing that is so dangerous about quitting is that it's so easy. Let me tell you a story.

I was raised by wonderful parents is Southern California. We were migrant farm workers and broke in terms of money my entire young life. But we were not broke in terms of love and support for each other. At age 12 I met Caesar Chavez and he became a hero of mine. I decided I wanted to be a civil rights attorney to work within the system to right injustices for my people. That is how I would be a soldier for right. I went into the U.S. Air Force and when I got out I went to Long Beach State University and began my studies.

Well, life takes strange twists and turns. It was suggested to me that an acting class would help my persuasive abilities in the courtroom and that it would be a good idea to take some drama as elective courses. I found something in those classes that I loved... attention! I really *liked* being the center of attention and I discovered that I was funny. I began to work at *The Comedy Store*, local comedy club, parking cars and doing a few minutes of stand-up when the owner could fit me in. Well, one night legendary producer Norman Lear came in to see someone else and also saw me. As a result I went from making $20 a night to being handed a bonus check for $75,000 with a salary of $35,000 a week just two weeks later! I didn't have enough I.D. to cash the bonus check! The people at the bank laughed me out of there!

A.K.A. Pablo was born and I was on my way...but to where? As the money got bigger, the parties got longer and more frequent until it seemed they never stopped. I began to change and become someone who lost the sense of values that my family had taught me. I lost my true friends, I caused my girl friend that I was planning to marry to leave me because of my lack of consideration. I was losing my grip as so called success came my way. The change was insidious because you don't realize it's happening. Then the show got canceled and everything came to a halt. I quit getting invitations to the A-list parties, no one was interested in yesterday's news, which is what I became overnight. At 26 years old people were asking me, "didn't you used to be...". That is not a good feeling. I hit a low that was profound. My girl friend found someone else and married, I was not allowed to play the *Comedy Store* because I was so rude to the owner when I was "on top", my new so-called friends quit coming around as soon as they found the show had been canceled.

So where do you go at a time like this? Home. My mom sat me down and told me "this can destroy you only if you let it. You have to believe that another opportunity will come. You're still the same guy that caught the eye of Norman Lear, you're still funny, this really changes nothing...*if* you're willing to learn form it and move on." She made me see that I had put all my eggs in one basket and that I thought I would be famous and rich forever. I saw how fast it changes. In this business nobody is famous forever unless you're George Burns or Lucille Ball! I got my life in order with the help of my mom and the Grace of God and I went out to ask forgiveness of everyone I had hurt with my thoughtlessness. In the difficult process I discovered something that totally humbles me. My true friends never left. They were there all the time. It was me who left them.

Since then, since the low of the cancellation of *A.K.A. Pablo*, I have had nothing but highs in my life. As you said Andy, I have a lot going on. Television, movies, writing and producing, and it is all because I know that success is in the journey. Doing your best and serving people with what you do. Stretching and growing and helping other people do the same throughout your life. Success isn't a place, it's a way of life and I am eternally gratefully that I had people around me that cared enough to help me re-focus when I needed it. In fact, I was recently given the honor of presenting Norman Lear the Lifetime Achievement Award, a very prestigious award here in Hollywood. In talking with him he confessed to me that he could have used his muscle to keep our show on another season. He had heard of how my life was going during that period and made a decision to let them cancel it. He said he didn't want me to become another sad Hollywood story. Funny isn't it, what seems like the worst thing that could happen turns out to be the best thing that could happen. *If*, like mom said, you're willing to learn from it and move on.

Keep 'em laughin', and learnin',

Paul Rodriguez

Paul Rodriguez

*"Whether you think you can
or think you can't –
you are right."*

Henry Ford

WOLFMAN JACK

DISC JOCKEY

...will be remembered for his 30 years on radio, television, and film. He was an American Original who is assured a place in rock 'n roll history.

No other voice was as familiar to millions around the world as Wolfman Jack's. He was an American original - a one of a kind entertainment personality whose three decades on radio, television and film have assured him a place in rock 'n roll history.

At the height of the Vietnam War, Wolfman Jack was the single most popular radio personality in the world. For more than ten years, he provided programming for servicemen and women around the globe on Armed Forces Radio. In 1973, George Lucas immortalized the Wolfman as a teen icon in his film "American Graffiti." It was the first time anyone had seen the "real" Wolfman, and his face soon became as recognizable as his voice.

Sadly, Wolfman Jack passed away shortly after his letter was received, leaving a void in the entertainment industry. The man will be greatly missed, but his accomplishments in the form of recordings and the lives he touched will go on forever.

A DIVISION OF WOLFMAN JACK INC.
ROUTE 1 #56 • BELVIDERE, NC 27919

Dear Andy,

Thanks for your letter. Yeah, I'd be really happy to share something from the ol' Wolfman's life with your readers. Just one request, though. Although there's sadness in my story, I want everyone to keep a light heart. Maybe they should pretend they really *are* Wolfman Jack while they read my story – use a crazy hipster voice and roll their eyes and wave an arm in the air when they hit the good parts, like they're really trying to reach out and communicate with somebody. Because that's half the fun of being who I am. And if there's anything a person ought to learn from my life, it's that even the most unhappy folks among us can find a way to turn their lives around.

Andy, you can't believe how cool it is that you should ask me to be in your book right now. As it turns out, I've just finishing writing the story of my life, which is gonna be called Have Mercy!. So I got my memories very alive at this moment.

The hardest part of writing my book was sorting through painful memories from when I was a kid. But it also made me realize that the pain I went through then was what set the stage for my becoming Wolfman Jack – a much more together person, with much more to offer the world than the bummed-out, broken-home, gang-joining, juvenile delinquent Brooklyn kid I used to be. Emotional pain forced me to look for a different world to be in. Once I found it, in the soulful, expressive black and black-inspired music that came through my radio, I began moving myself into that world. As a result, I've had some incredible experiences, and spent my life being close to the music I love, and the people who make the music.

I was born into a family of very special and talented people. One of my grandfathers was a college professor. My old man, Weston Smith, was a millionaire businessman. At least, up until the stock market crash, which happened nine years before I was born. My older sister, Joan, was – still is – a smart and gorgeous woman who gave up a real promising modeling career to marry a great, successful guy and raise terrific children. But, for all the good things my family had going for it, we also ran up against bad luck.

After the crash, my dad struggled real hard to try to regain his earlier prosperity, working any job he could get, two jobs at a time whenever he could. And he did great, but never up to the standards he'd set for himself. He and my mother had great love for each other, but somehow their relationship strained to its breaking point when I was about six years old.

At the time my folks split up, I had two best friends. One was my sister. The other was our family's maid, Frances, a really divine black lady who loved us even more than we loved our own selves. Besides being constantly sweet and affectionate, she was the first person to give me a taste of black music, one of the most important influences in my whole life. Joan and I would cuddle up with Frances on Sunday mornings and we'd all listen to the radio together, to gorgeous black spirituals, music just full of love and energy, endurance and hope.

About a year later, my parents each got re-married. Both new spouses didn't like me very much, whether out of jealousy or meanness, I'll never know. I was divided between two different households, both of them real troubled. The whole emotional atmosphere of my young life got colder. I mostly recall a lot of distance, a lot of being-in-control power trips coming from my new step-parents.

Our maid Frances' heart was broken by all this discord. Earlier, she stuck with the family even when we couldn't afford to pay her wages. But it hurt her too much to see the family torn apart. All her love wasn't enough to counteract that scene. Not long after she had left, my sister got married. Her husband's career as a Navy officer took them both hundreds of miles away.

I was a very downhearted kid, very alone, dealing with more hostility than I could understand. I found a dog on the street and it became my new best friend. I called him Rags. One day, my stepmother poisoned him. I did poorly in school, not because I was stupid, but because I was *discouraged*. I didn't see any point in trying. As I got older, I got into a spiral of trouble. I *wanted* to be bad. Joining a gang led to a rumble where I got some front teeth knocked out. My closest buddy - who would later on spend some serious penitentiary time - could hot-wire cars. So we stole a different car and went joy-riding almost every afternoon, until one day the cops busted up our show and hauled us in.

Along the way, I got bounced from one strict school to another, earmarked for "vocational" training, then for emotional problems.

But during those same years I also kept doing something real positive, something that would eventually unlock my future. To me, it was just having fun. To my folks, it was a big waste of time, but at least it kept me off the streets.

One day my dad gave me a powerful radio, which I took down into the coal bin area of the Brooklyn apartment where we lived. Late at night, my buddies and I could get some real unusual stuff on that radio, faraway broadcasts from Tennessee and Texas, and unfamiliar close-by areas like Harlem. The wilder a program was, the more we loved it. Most of all, we dug the be-boppin', hip-talkin' rhythm and blues disc jockeys. They had great personalities, a solid sense of cool, and exactly the kind of job we all wanted to have. Because we were headed for crummy jobs, and we knew it.

This was just before rock & roll became an important part of the music business. Folks called it rhythm and blues then, and not many white people would listen to it. Most of these DJs who impressed me were black. A few, I learned later, were white guys who loved black music and culture so much that they dove right into it, headfirst. One of the greatest was John R., from WLAC in Nashville. He was so authentic, and the music he played was so soul-moving, that some black folks in the south even named their *children* after him.

Lo and behold, one day I also got my hands on a primitive little tape recorder, a reel-to-reel job. My buddies and I down in the coal bin would record the coolest DJ's, like Symphony Sid, or Jocko, who started each show like it was the blast-off of a rocket ship. Then we'd practice talking like our idols. It turned out that I was pretty good at it. Pretty soon, instead of cutting school to hang out with a gang, I was cutting school to spend my time learning radio at a black music station. I'd do anything to make those folks want me around - run to the corner store for sandwiches, sweep up, anything to be useful. The people were appreciative. They started teaching me. An engineer explained the control board, even let me work the switches. One night, that engineer called in sick. I got to actually *run* the board for Mr. Blues, a DJ I idolized. That was heaven.

Playing hooky at the radio station eventually brought about a nasty blow-up between my stepmother and me. I was just barely old enough to go out on my own, and pretty eager to escape anyway. So I took off. Needless to say, I didn't have a high school diploma.

After a whole lot of dead-end jobs and getting into various scrapes, one day I focused again on my dream of being a DJ. I got it together enough to enroll in a radio broadcast school in Washington, D.C., near where I was living then.

The school was a prestige joint, with an emphasis on classical music. Me, I was whole hog for rhythm and blues. And in those days, among white folks, people thought that was a real dangerous, wrong-side-of-the-tracks enthusiasm to have. So I was still an outsider. But, because I'd dreamed so long about being a DJ, and practiced it down in the basement, and gotten myself hands-on training from professional radio people, I absolutely thrived at that school. All my former teachers at all the problem-kid schools would've cried for joy to see me doing that straight-A work, being the leader in class projects. On the side, I completed my high school education and got that diploma, too.

The lady who ran the radio school didn't understand where I was coming from, but she respected how hard I worked. She introduced me to an adventuresome station owner who programmed his stations for black audiences. That man gave me my first radio job, working a struggling little station in Newport News that only employed two DJs. My co-worker there, a brilliant, Harvard-educated black man, completed my education on black music and style. Inspired, I eventually went to invent a character called Wolfman Jack. Then I gradually *became* that character.

All of this had happened by my mid-twenties, and my life has been a rush of excitement ever since: working with great performers, several years as host of The Midnight Special, getting featured in George Lucas's first movie, American Graffiti, being on over a thousand radio stations at a time, spreading a message of love and joy to the men and women stationed in Viet Nam, just countless great memories.

People have loved this Wolfman Jack character so much, he's still going strong after three decades in show business. In fact, recently I've been enjoying some of my best times ever.

Is there a message in all this? Well, I latched on to something I loved, found joy in it, and I did whatever I could to get involved - even though at that time it wasn't socially approved for white people to openly admire the art and the style of black people. The strife I knew as a kid hurt me, but also focused me more. People in my own home said I would turn out to be a bum. And I almost proved them right. Until I got back on track with my original dream. And now I get to make people happy, using inspiration from the great radio personalities who touched me when I was young. With the help of a wonderful woman who has always stuck by me, through many ups and downs, I've also enjoyed a long-lasting marriage, raising two great kids.

Andy, what I've told your readers about in this letter isn't the *only* storm of my life. There've been plenty more. I've been locked up in jail, and I've also been on top of the world. Sometimes success made my head too big and caused me to make a fool of myself. But a force has always lead me back home, and straightened out my course in life: I love what I do and I love the people around me.

I suspect the same thing is true in your own life. I dig your books. They help people, inspire them through tough times. That just makes me want to throw back my head and give a big wolf howl in your honor.

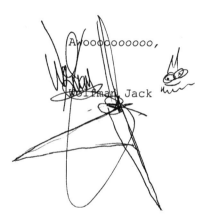

Awoooooooooo,

Wolfman Jack

JIMMY WALKER

ENTREPRENEUR

...is the founder of Jimmy Walker and Associates, Ltd. insurance company. Today the company has over 2,500 clients and represents approximately 150 professional athletes and entertainers.

Jimmy Walker has spanned two arenas of athletics and business; reaching the highest and lowest points in both... Jimmy is now a major business success but has vivid memories of being broke and owing millions to his creditors. He was also once a gifted college basketball player, but found himself falling short of the talent to play professional ball.

Jimmy merged his love of athletics and business to form a career selling insurance to many of the world's most famous athletes. Stars such as Chris Evert, Michael Jordan, Bill Walton and Bobby Riggs all publicly praise Jimmy for his business creativity, honesty and superior service. Jimmy has become enormously successful.

Jimmy quotes George Shinn by saying, "There is no such thing as a self-made man. You reach your goals with the help of others." Jimmy's attitude of generosity is demonstrated by his participation in a favorite charity: Bicycles for Kids. This program, during the past 12 years, has given approximately 2,000 bicycles to underprivileged children. The bikes are given away at Christmas parties held at Jimmy's home.

Jimmy Walker & Associates, Ltd.

The Esplanade / 2425 E. Camelback, Suite 885 / Phoenix, AZ 85016
(602) 956-7111 / Facsimile (602) 956-5653
9441 Wilshire Blvd. / Beverly Hills, CA 90212

Andy Andrews
P. O. Box 17321
Nashville, TN 37217

Dear Andy,

Thanks for the opportunity to share some thoughts in your new book.

The success which I have enjoyed in life didn't come easy or quickly. When I was younger I had a life long dream of playing professional basketball, although my accomplishments playing basketball at Arizona State University clearly indicated that my skills were not NBA caliber. Fortunately, I was able to take that disappointment and use it as a positive motivation to pursue the insurance business following college and it's been a business that I've enjoyed since 1966.

I experienced a financial set-back in life in the late 1970's when I owned the Phoenix Racquets in World Team Tennis. I became the sole General Partner and signed Chris Evert to play on the Phoenix Racquets Tennis Team. Although our franchise led the League in attendance and I was named World Team Tennis Executive of the Year, we were still losing substantial dollars.

My financial losses, over several years of Professional Tennis, accumulated in excess of $1 Million and my challenges at the age of 28 were huge! My accountants and attorneys tried to convince me that the only way out was to file for bankruptcy. Each time I left a meeting with my advisors I was more determined than ever to prove that they were wrong, since I had a very strong commitment to pay every debt where I had a personal obligation.

I found that Joshua 1:9 has served as a source of encouragement for me when it says, "Be strong and courageous, do not tremble or be dismayed, for the Lord your God is with you wherever you go." The strength and wisdom I have received from the Lord, along with plenty of support from my wife and family, helped me to retire every debt without going through legal channels, such as bankruptcy, with my professional tennis investment.

I've learned through the grace of God to roll with the punches and sometimes in life it's impossible to change the circumstances of many different types of problems that continue to come into our lives, although we certainly have the ability to change our attitudes and I believe that anything is possible with a willing and positive heart.

Andy, I'm still learning everyday in life that the impossible can become possible when we are able to see the obstacles as opportunities which can allow us to grow, especially when we are faced with adversity.

It's my understanding that Winston Churchill's most famous speech was only ten words and it was delivered to a graduating class. Churchill's message was "Never Give Up. Never Give Up. Never, Never Give Up!" Following Churchill's speech of only ten words he immediately sat down and then received a standing ovation!

In closing, I'm confident that I have learned more wisdom from my financial failure in tennis than any financial success I have ever received in the insurance business. Today our company has written almost $600 Million of life insurance throughout the past 30 years and we presently represent approximately 150 professional athletes, along with various business people, primarily helping many of our clients to discount their estate tax cost.

Thanks, Andy, for allowing me to share some thoughts and I hope it will strengthen and support some of your readers during the tough times which we all face when we feel like tossing in the towel!

All the Best,

Jimmy Walker

JW:jat

*"The only thing that stands
between a man and what he
wants from life is often
merely the will to try it and
the faith to believe that
it is possible."*

Richard M. DeVos

LOU FERRIGNO

ACTOR

...is well known in the circles of body building. His physique and personality immediately landed him the role as the "Incredible Hulk." Lou has a constantly expanding acting and business career.

Lou Ferrigno has ventured far from his early beginnings as television's Incredible Hulk. Since then, Lou has enjoyed a succession of roles in television, movies and live theater.

As the youngest and only man in history to win the coveted Mr. Universe title two years in a row. Lou displays his 6'4", 255 pound stature as a testament to discipline and determination. In 1974 alone, he won the titles for Mr. Teenage America, Mr. America, Mr. Universe and Mr. International. This established Lou as a mainstay in worldwide bodybuilding competitions.

Now, as an actor, Lou Ferrigno is able to display a vulnerability that amazes even the most seasoned professionals. His letter gives us a clue to this ability. A childhood marked by low self esteem and a lifetime of commitment to change can provide an actor with an arsenal of emotions.

Lou Ferrigno Enterprises, Inc.

Andy Andrews
P.O.Box 2761
Gulf Shores, Alabama 36547

Dear Andy,

  The things that are our greatest obstacles are often things that seem small, almost insignificant, in our lives. I am convinced that sometimes these things are so seemingly inconsequential that we have relegated them to a place in our minds that is all but forgotten. Yet they continue to control and shape our actions and reactions and determine our futures.

  When I was born I had an inner ear infection that went undetected until I lost 85% of my hearing. That in itself wasn't what shaped my early personality, however. It was my father's reaction to my impairment. He was a good provider, but because he was a tough police officer dealing on a daily basis with tough situations, he maintained a defensive stance against the world. In a sense, for him, my problem was something to "fight." As a young boy this translated to me as an absence of love. So, because of a series of esteem crushing incidents with him and others, I became very introverted. I was living totally within myself.

  Ironically, my first recollection of an interest in body building was of my father who was always in great shape. He came out of the bath with a towel wrapped around his waist into the kitchen. He saw me looking at his physique. "Hey Louie, watch this !", he said and struck a double-biceps pose. He was awesome and I realized then what could be done with the human body if you refused to let yourself go. I knew that this was something I could do. It was something I could learn about and do quietly, within myself.

  The most important thing that came out of this interest was that I realized this was *something I could do to change.* And I *wanted* to change. If you want to change and take the responsibility of that change upon yourself, you will prevail... even over a lifetime of things that continually say you can't! Step by step I developed as an athlete and emerged to be one of the most decorated competitors in the sport, winning titles of Mr. America, Mr. Universe and Mr. International. I have starred in movies and television and written a book to help others learn through my experience. I came back as a 41 year old to compete for the title of Mr. Olympia. You see, Andy, age also is not a factor when you decide to make your body the servant of your mind! Currently my wife, Carla, and I are enjoying life. I am acting as a personal trainer to top individuals in sports, politics and movies as I pursue filming and working in the motion picture industry full time.

  Finally, Andy, I have come to believe success is a combination of a true desire to change and a willingness to work. You can overcome huge obstacles and achieve your dreams with these two ingredients and a healthy supplement of persistence.

Sincerely,

Lou Ferrigno

Lou Ferrigno

P.O. Box 1671 • Santa Monica, California 90406 • Telephone: 310/395-2144

IRVING R. LEVINE

NEWSCASTER

...is one of the most renowned and respected journalists in broadcasting. At present, he is based in Washington, DC, and serves as Chief Economics Correspondent for NBC.

Irving R. Levine, an NBC News correspondent for more than 40 years, is one of the most renowned and respected journalists in broadcasting. He has reported and interpreted fast-breaking news and major economic, political and social trends on television and radio on four continents. *Time* magazine has called him the "pioneer" of economics reporting on television. At present, he is based in Washington, D.C. and serves Chief Economics Correspondent.

The first network correspondent to cover economics full time, Irving reports on financial trends and the marketplace, taxation and tariffs, and money: who has it, who doesn't, and what are they doing with it. Irving has accompanied Presidents Ford, Carter, Reagan, Bush and Clinton to the annual economic summit meetings in Puerto Rico, Tokyo, Bonn, Paris, Ottawa, Toronto, Versailles, Venice, Williamsburgh, Munich, Houston and London. He has traveled to Beijing and Shanghai with the Secretary of the Treasury to cover the start of United States-China trade negotiations.

Prior to his current assignment in the nation's capital, Irving was an NBC News correspondent for four years in Moscow, 10 years in Rome, two years in Tokyo and a year in London. As a war correspondent, he covered the Korean conflict and the truce talks at Panmunjom for NBC News. In Rome, he reported on the Vatican's Ecumenical Council, and he accompanied Pope Paul VI on his historic flights to Jerusalem, Bombay and elsewhere. In Moscow, he broadcast reports on the events of the Krushchev era following Stalin's rule. He was the first television network correspondent accredited in the Soviet Union.

4001 Nebraska Avenue, N.W.
Washington, D.C. 20016
202 885-4200

A Division of
National Broadcasting
Company, Inc.

Andy Andrews
P.O. Box 2761
Gulf Shores, Alabama 36547

Dear Andy:

Thank you for asking me to contribute some thoughts based on personal experience on overcoming obstacles and setbacks in life.

I can offer no better advice, based on my own career, than that spoken often by my mother when I was growing up in Pawtucket, Rhode Island.

My mother's constant counsel was that "bottom is more important than brains."

What she meant was that to achieve worthwhile goals in life and to overcome defeats and reverses along the way, one must be willing to apply "bottom" -- that is to set one's "bottom" down and patiently take the time to work through problems rather than to flee from them.

In short, perserverance was more essential than intelligence.

An early confirmation of the wisdom of this advice came shortly after high school when I was accepted at Brown University, but my parents lacked the financial means to pay for the tuition and other expenses.

This put my mother's aphorism to the test. Whatever I.Q. had gotten me admitted to Brown, it would take "bottom" to apply myself to jobs, in a depressed economy, to finance my education. At the same time it would take "bottom" to sit through the long hours of study to make the most of the educational opportunity.

Perserverance paid. I found parttime work wherever I could -- at a soda fountain, in a shoe store, as a chauffeur, as a shipyard guard, babysitting. At the same time, devoting long hours to cracking the books which won me a Phi Beta Kappa key in my junior year at Brown.

In the years that followed, in the army in World War II, as an NBC news correspondent during the Korean War and in Russia and many other places, that early experience served as a constant reminder in confronting the inevitable, and often more daunting, roadblocks and pitfalls along the way.

Perserverance and patience, bottom more than brains: keeping this is mind had been an important key in whatever success I've achieved.

With best wishes to you and your readers,

Sincerely,

Irving R. Levine
NBC News
Chief Economics Correspondent

LEONARD NIMOY

ACTOR

...is widely known as "Mr. Spock" from the "Star Trek" television series. Leonard is also a successful movie director and producer.

Whether you are "Trekkie" or not, everyone is familiar with Spock, and the man, Leonard Nimoy, who portrayed this character while captivating millions of Americans with the adventures of the Enterprise and her crew. Leonard Nimoy's acting prowess has been evident; not only in the episodes of "Star Trek," but also in TV's "Mission Impossible," and his narrations for "In Search Of" and his several motion pictures.

Leonard has certainly achieved success beyond his portrayal of Spock or other characters. He has displayed as much skill in writing, directing and producing movies. His contributions as a story writer and executive producer are evident in the Star Trek IV and VI films. He has also directed such feature films as "Three Men and a Baby," "Funny About Love" and "Holy Matrimony." He has also been nominated for several Emmy awards. Perhaps less generally known, Leonard Nimoy has written three volumes of poetry and recorded ten narrative albums.

One would think a man of Leonard's talents would have made a quick impression upon his appearance in the acting arena. This was far from the case. Without Leonard's persistence to follow his dream, his abilities would have remained hidden and none of us would have had the pleasure of enjoying the entertainment he has provided for all of us.

Leonard Nimoy

Dear Andy:

Thanks for asking. It's hard for people to
grasp the idea that "overnight" stardom is a
myth created by Hollywood publicity
departments.

Hard work and persistence are much more often
the truth of our lives. When I first arrived
in Hollywood I had a tough time finding
representation, let alone an acting job.
During my first 15 years in my business, I
never had an acting job that lasted longer
than two weeks! That meant constantly
looking for work and being turned down again
and again until "Star Trek" came along, but
when it did, I had done my homework, "paid my
dues" and was ready.

During the tough times I often sustained
myself by reciting a poem called "Invictus"
(Invincible).

The first stanza is:

        Out of the night that covers me
        black as a pit from pole to pole,
        I thank whatever Gods may be
        for my unconquerable soul.

Best,

Leonard Nimoy

VIC CONANT

BUSINESSMAN

...is president of the Nightingale-Conant Corporation. The corporation is the world's leader in producing business and personal development audio programming.

As president of Nightingale-Conant Corporation, Vic Conant both teaches and experiences phenomenal success. Nightingale-Conant, based in Niles, Illinois, is the world's undisputed leader in producing business and personal development audio programming. The corporation sells more than seven million audiocassettes each year.

Vic has headed the company since 1986, when his father, co-founder Lloyd Conant, passed away. Lloyd's fellow co-founder and long-time business partner was Earl Nightingale, whose "The Strangest Secret" received the first ever Gold Record - representing one million copies sold - given to a spoken word recording.

Vic credits these two visionary pioneers with creating the foundation of success on which his company is based. And he vows to continue that vision. New product development is key to the vision and remains an ongoing concern, one that in recent years has seen Nightingale-Conant move into the ever expanding markets of video, books and other motivational products.

Because of its international reputation as "the shortest distance between where you are and where you could be," for 35 years tens of million men and women have turned to Nightingale-Conant to help themselves achieve the greatest possible success in their professional and personal lives.

With a stable of speakers and authors that includes such business greats as Tom Peters, Brian Tracy, Roger Dawson, Jay Abraham and Denis Waitley, and inspirational masters like Dr. Wayne Dyer, Zig Ziglar, Leo Buscaglia and Deepak Chopra, M.D., Nightingale-Conant Corporation - with Vic at the helm - seems destined to enjoy at least another 35 years of spectacular success.

Nightingale Conant

OFFICE OF THE PRESIDENT

Andy Andrews
P.O. Box 2761
Gulf Shores, AL 36547

Dear Andy,

The lessons we can all glean from the letters in your book are certainly useful in any endeavor. I thank you for thinking of Nightingale-Conant and me in your effort. My particular story actually begins and ends with the family-owned Nightingale-Conant business. Fortunately it has a happy ending. However my wife and I had a period of struggle in the middle portion of our journey.

After I returned from the service, in my mid-twenties, I went to work for my father and Earl Nightingale in their joint business, Nightingale-Conant. Also working with me was Earl's son, Dave. After about a year the company found itself going through some very hard times. The sales techniques we were using weren't working, and as a result both Dave and I were let go. My wife's parents were living in Florida, so we picked ourselves up and took this as an exciting time to pursue other opportunities. In fact, I wanted to go into commercial real estate which, at that time, was very lucrative in Florida. Once in Florida I discovered that the state required a year's residency before you could apply for a real estate license. So I went to work selling cars, which turned out to be great training and a pretty good living. After 12 months passed I was ready to carry out my real estate plan.

As life would have it, however, my entry into real estate coincided with the major recession of 1973. Interest rates skyrocketed, fueled by the oil embargo. Real estate and my wife and I (she had entered the field as well) took it on the chin. It was a terrible time for many people. Banks folded, people lost lifetime investments and the entire industry collapsed. We had purchased a nice home preparing for the prosperity we felt was just around the corner. I was trying to sell apartment complexes and my wife was trying to sell waterfront condominiums for the next year. That year our combined incomes were a couple thousand dollars! We were sinking fast. We had to sell our home and move into an apartment complex. In fact, I had made friends with the apartment complex owner, and he let us live in a unit rent-free as long as we managed the complex for him. This was a blessing, but a far cry from where we had hoped to be by this time.

Then, again as life would have it, I came across an old recording as I was packing to move. It was called *The Science of Getting Rich* by Wallace D. Wattle. The book that the recording was taken from was written in the early 1900s. The message I heard was metaphysical in nature and affected me very strongly.

NIGHTINGALE-CONANT CORPORATION
7300 North Lehigh Avenue • Niles, Illinois 60714 • FAX 1-708-647-7145 • Phone 1-708-647-0300

Andy Andrews
Page 2

It related the basic truth that you can control your destiny by
focusing on the things you desire and going after them with
single-minded clarity. At the time I was working on our home in
preparation to attempt to sell it. Remember, the bottom had
fallen out of the real estate market. Nothing was selling. This
was the *worst* time to try to sell a home. But I decided to
experiment with the idea I had heard on the tape. As I worked on
the house, and in every spare minute I had, I began visualizing
the sale. I focused my mental energy on a consistent basis
toward that end. In two weeks it sold for the full asking price!
I was stunned.

I decided to try this again. This time I would put the
energy into landing a good job. I had done my research and had
chosen the field of medical supply sales as the area to pursue.
I had chosen Zimmer USA as the optimum medical supply company.
So I called on the regional rep, told him that I had decided to
work for his company and basically "here I am." We talked, but
he finally told me there were no openings. To which I replied,
"Well, I'm sorry but I've decided to work for your company and
there is nothing you can do about it!" I kept calling on him
every two weeks for six months. My wife and I had even begun to
wonder if *we* were crazy. Well, he never hired me but he talked
to a friend of his who had a distributorship in Chicago. His
friend called me with an offer, which I accepted. Later we
learned through a series of conversations that he knew my father.
Several other "coincidences" left us feeling like it was a match
that was meant to be.

The principles I heard on the recording obviously worked.
They gave me hope during a somewhat desperate time. They also
gave me a path to positive action, which led us out of the fear
and the paralysis that fear can cause. Later I rejoined my
father and Nightingale-Conant, as did Dave Nightingale. The
company is now international and growing at a healthy pace.

Reviewing my journey to this point, Andy, I believe the key
is to never lose sight of the fact that *we can control* the
ultimate outcome of our life situation. In other words, learning
to control and focus our thoughts toward the ends we desire will
unlock an ability to recognize the opportunities that will lead
us there and give us the energy we need to take advantage of
those opportunities. As I said, it certainly worked for me. But
the best news of all is that it will work for anyone! Thanks
again, Andy, for your kind invitation to be included in *Storms of
Perfection III*.

All the best,

Vic Conant

VC:mr

"The greatest power that a person possesses is the power to choose."

J. Marlin Kohe

SALLY ANN STEWART

JOURNALIST

...is a seasoned journalist with a proven track record. Sally survived the Northridge earthquake that struck LA on January 17, 1994.

It's not every day you lose your home, your neighbors and your life's savings. It all happened to Sally Ann Stewart in one day. In fact, it all happened in about 30 seconds on the morning of January 17, 1994, when the powerful Northridge earthquake devastated the Los Angeles area.

Sally Ann Stewart is a USA Today reporter based in Los Angeles. She is a seasoned national journalist with a proven track record and broad-based experience in covering news. She finds the news and creates the stories from the west coast. If you read about the Rodney King or O.J. Simpson trials in USA Today, the articles were written by Sally Ann Stewart.

The Northridge earthquake encapsulated Sally as part of the news and not just as one present to cover the story. Her circumstances were changed in an instant from comfort to chaos. In 30 seconds, the massive quake killed 61 people and caused $20 billion in damage.

Sally's situation was shared by many. Her uplifting attitude should also be shared by many.

Sally Ann Stewart

Mr. Andy Andrews
P.O. Box 2761
Gulf Shores, AL 36547

Dear Andy,

Out here in southern California, as long as our homes don't get swept away by sliding mud, we love a ferocious rainstorm. It's a good excuse to skip the after-work jog, order in a pizza and watch a whole night of TV reruns. But the best part of the storm is the next morning, when the smog is washed away and you can see past the freeways and the billboards all the way to the mountains. It's so clear that you feel like you're sitting on top of the peak.

I've been thinking about that ever since you wrote to me, asking me to tell you how I've survived life's storms to live such a charmed life.

Nobody thinks that problems, rejection and anguish are fun. Once you've endured, though, you have a new respect for yourself. You know you climbed that hurdle and now you can enjoy the view. Maybe you even end up with a good story to tell. And, of course, there's nothing I love more than a good story.

My own story starts with Mom, Dad, four sisters and two brothers. Seven kids. The good part about growing up in a large family is that there's always someone who'll play with you. The not-so-good part is that no matter how many siblings you have, there's still only one Mom and one Dad. So you learn early on how to tie your own shoes, put on your own Band-Aid, fix your own sandwich, earn your own money and take care of yourself when you get out into the world.

From the time I taught myself how to read, I knew I wanted to tell stories. When I entered the University of Florida, I thought I'd graduate with a teaching degree, rent a room in an attic somewhere and write a novel that would be instantly recognized as Great. But then I figured that if what I really wanted to do was write, why spend a whole day teaching when I could get paid for doing what I love. That's when I showed up at the offices for the independent Florida Alligator, the nation's first truly independent, student-run college newspaper.

My first story was far from Great. In fact, the editor-in-chief re-wrote it, top to bottom. But I learned more than just how to do it better next time. I learned to take criticism with a touch of grace. And I learned that the worst rejection would be giving up and leaving a dream to die.

I never gave up. I got tapped for a sought-after internship at the Fort Lauderdale News after I told the editor that I was sure he could find a better reporter or a better writer than me but he'd never find anyone who worked harder. When I got it in my head to move to Washington, I knocked on every door at the National Press Club. Most of those doors stayed locked and bolted. But those didn't matter because one cracked open and I pushed it open the rest of the way to win my dream. And when I wanted to work for USA Today, I kept calling the managing editor. Now, Bob Dubill jokes that hiring me was the only way he could give his message-takers a rest.

In the past several years, I've learned how to keep forging ahead when the obstacles in front of me are of a more personal nature. When my brother, Michael, was killed in a drunk driving crash seven years ago, I thought I'd never get through a day without crying. And I didn't for a long time. I miss my brother every single day and even now, I wish I had the power to turn back the clock and change his fate.

On January 17, 1994, the Northridge earthquake destroyed the first home I'd ever bought. In just 30 seconds, most of my possessions were shattered, my neighborhood was devastated and my life's savings were gone.

Believe it or not, though, there was a lot of good that came out of that disaster. I have the happiness of knowing that my friends came through for me. Jeff went into my condo in the dark the night after the earthquake because I remembered I'd left Michael's picture behind. Blythe opened her home to me and my few boxes of salvaged belongings. Gary and Carol took care of my cat, Libby, for a month. Susan took a day off from work to go apartment hunting with me. Linda helped me make an insurance list of my losses by walking around a department store with me, so I could see everything I used to own. My sister, Barbara, packed her toolbox and flew to Los Angeles to help make my new apartment feel like a home.

The earthquake also gave me a chance to help others, like the woman who owned the neighborhood perfume store. She lost most of her stock in the earthquake and there wasn't any insurance. So I bought a bottle of perfume and told a friend, who bought a bottle of perfume and told her friend, and so it went.

And, as all of us helped each other pull our lives back together, we learned that stuff is just stuff. So it felt natural when we all piled into my apartment for a party celebrating the one-year anniversary of the earthquake. We talked about the good things the earthquake brought to us. We toasted our good fortune for surviving what many people didn't. We know we may have lost nearly everything we owned on January 17, 1994, but we're holding on to each other for our lifetimes.

The earthquake even gave me my new motto. When the dust settled a bit, I took a break from quake repair to go to Hawaii for a week of rest. While rummaging through a Waikiki art fair in the pouring rain, I found a rubber stamp with the Chinese character for Happiness on it. I was reaching for my wallet when I saw another rubber stamp, this one bearing the characters for Double Happiness.

That's what I strive for now. To me, happiness is something that shows on your face, like when you're having a good laugh. But Double Happiness means you also have happiness in your soul because you're living, learning and loving the best that you can.

Sometimes, it seems to me that I started my career thinking that hard work was the path that would bring me to all my goals. I still believe hard work matters, but now, from my perch on top of this mountain, I see that I have the opportunity to find out what happens when I add a strong dose of Double Happiness.

With warmest regards and best wishes for Double Happiness,

Sally

Sally Ann Stewart

囍

DOUBLE HAPPINESS

*"You are where you are
today because you have
chosen to be there."*

Harry Browne

STEVE BARTKOWSKI

FORMER NFL QUARTERBACK

...was the NFL's highest rated quarterback for three years. Steve enjoys the outdoors, flying and public speaking.

Steve Bartkowski was the number one draft pick for the NFL in 1975. He had already been visited by great success in his young football career. Because of his exceptional athletic prowess, Steve had the luxury of choosing from 100 scholarships when he opted to attend the University of California at Berkeley to play football and baseball. After a brilliant college football career, Steve was the hottest new prospect in NFL football.

Steve Bartkowski is remembered for his attitude and approach to the game. He was a quarterback who commanded respect from his opponents and teammates alike. He delivered thrills and many victories for the Atlanta Falcons and later for the LA Rams. Steve is now a member of the "Quarterback Legends," an elite association of former NFL quarterbacks.

Steve has attained many career milestones. He has carried over his winning attitude and traits from his successful football career into a business career. He is President and CEO of Bart Productions Inc., an independent television production company providing outdoor programming to the television industry. Steve is now an avid golfer with a scratch handicap, and still lives in Atlanta with his wife, Sandee, and their two sons, Philip and Peter.

Mr. Andy Andrews
P. O. Box 2761
Gulf Shores, AL 36547

Dear Andy:

What a great privilege to be asked by you to chronicle an especially trying time in my life for your new book . . . . The hardest part of this endeavor has been selecting just <u>one</u> out of so many. I can say with great resolve that adversity has been a faithful tutor throughout my life.

I have discovered that once I'm firmly planted on solid ground on the backside of any of life's traumas, there have been valuable lessons learned which have served to build and shape character. There always seems to be a quantifiable advance through adversity.

One particular example of this took place in 1978. After being first pick in the NFL Draft of 1975, I had suffered through three seasons of injuries (an elbow and back-to-back knee surgeries) which had hampered my efforts to substantiate my draft status. Going into my fourth season I was finally physically healthy and ready to make my mark on the Game. The long months in rehabilitation for my injured knee were but a distant memory yielding to the excitement of a new season. As training camp opened, I felt that I was in the best shape of my life - and raring to get on with the games.

Well, my enthusiasm was soon swallowed up by my poor showing in the first couple exhibition games. . . . . . the harder I tried the worse things got. Finally, in pre-season game number five, I played so badly that I lost my job to a free-agent quarterback from Portland State named June Jones, III. For the first time in my life I would not be the #1 guy. . . . . . . the NFL season would open with me as a *spectator*. This was the all-time low point of my life.

3400 CORPORATE WAY • SUITE G • DULUTH, GEORGIA 30136
(404) 623-0825   Fax (404) 623-3060

After getting over the initial trauma - thanks be to God - I was able to take an in-depth look at my life and where I was going. The picture was not very pretty. I knew there would have to be some very serious changes made if I was ever to experience life to the fullest. The problem was that I was powerless to make those changes and I needed some serious help. That's when I surrendered my life to God - the one who had given me life to begin with. From that moment of decision, changes began to happen which literally affected my entire life - including football.

I had my job back in a couple of weeks and went on to experience a great year in 1978 and a productive 12 year career in the NFL. I know that I would never have had the opportunity to succeed had it not been for that one pivotal moment in time when I was able to clearly see a more definitive purpose for my life than I'd ever seen before.

As the years have passed, I find that I look at adversity in a much different light. Life seems to be full of disappointments and, at times, it is easy to get "down" under these weighty moments; but, my faith has taught me to press on through, run the good race, and to finish the course. . . . . and endeavor to see disappointments as *His* appointments.

Andy, thanks so much for allowing me to be a part of this wonderful project. All the best to you, my friend.

Sincerely,

Steve Bartkowski

"As I grow older, I pay less attention to what men say. I just watch what they do."

Andrew Carnegie

Keith Thibodeaux

KEITH THIBODEAUX

ACTOR

...is known to millions of "I Love Lucy" fans as "Little Ricky Ricardo." Keith has written his autobiography, Life After Lucy.

Hailed as a child prodigy, Keith began playing drums at the age of two. His incredible abilities thrust him into the midst of a national Big-Band tour at the tender age of three. He starred as "Little Ricky" on "I Love Lucy" for four seasons and also acted in a number of other TV shows; including Opie's best pal on "The Andy Griffith Show." But Keith's early stardom and label of "Little Ricky" was a mixed blessing.

Keith could not shed his reputation of being "Little Ricky," and found it difficult to be known for his own identity, especially while growing up in high school. Keith's parents separated when he was 15, and he began looking for an escape. Like many child stars, Keith found himself adrift as a young adult and suffered depression and thoughts of suicide. He found his escape in drugs and rock 'n roll bands.

Keith credits his turn around to his conversion to Christianity and to wonderful wife Kathy. He is now an executive director of the national touring ballet company "Ballet Magnificat," founded by Kathy (an Olympic silver medalist in the 1982 International Ballet Competition).

M*a̶gnificat!* Ballet

5406 I-55 North
Jackson, MS 39211-4094
(601) 977-1001 / FAX: (601) 977-8948

Dear Andy,

Thanks for asking me to be part of your inspiring book.

When I was a drummer in Lafayette, Louisiana, years after the "I Love Lucy Show" was over, I learned about a formidable thing I call "the wall." The wall is the barrier that separates us from the next level we want to achieve in life. It may be a wall associated with the playing of a musical instrument. It can be a wall of defeat hanging over you.

In my case, I saw myself playing the drums at a certain level of excellence, but could not physically execute it because of the gap between what I wanted to be able to do and the limitations of my current ability. But, I kept at it and kept at it. I distinctly remember the day I broke through that wall -- I'll never forget it! I actually began performing on that level of excellence, not just aspiring toward it. But, I had to see myself there first.

The important thing to remember about that wall is: it's not just one wall, but can be many walls. In a way, it's frustrating -- but, if you get to the next level, it's worth it! I recently told my daughter, who is an excellent ballet dancer, about the wall in front of her. She wanted to see herself doing all these great things with ballet, but she couldn't physically execute them.

I told her that she <u>has</u> to get to the next level and break through that wall. To do that, you have to have persistence, and a realization that there's a barrier in front of you which must come down. Work, work, work!

The key is to recognize that there is a wall in front of you, and that its purpose is to challenge you to take that next step. Then, one day, you'll wake up and realize that you have indeed reached the next level. Nothing comes easy, but with God's help, I will get through that next wall!

Sincerely,

Keith Thibodeaux

Keith Thibodeaux

"Let them praise His name with dancing." Psalm 149:3

KEN KRAGEN

**PERSONAL MANAGER/
TELEVISION PRODUCER**

*...has spent more than 30 years
in the entertainment business.
Ken was the creator and organizer of the "We Are The World"
African relief effort.*

I have had the good fortune of knowing Ken Kragen for over 10 years. Ken has a warm personality that seems to draw people to him, and a skillful apti- tude to see a project through to its' successful conclusion. His attributes have been recognized and tapped into by several entertainers to promote their own careers.

Ken has been the cog in the wheel of success for several major undertak- ings. We have all been able to enjoy the efforts of a "behind the scenes" organi- zation that facilitated the success of such stars as Kenny Rogers, Lionel Richie, Olivia Newton-John, Burt Reynolds, Travis Tritt, Trisha Yearwood, The Limelighters and the Smothers Brothers. Ken has even taught a weekly course in personal management at the University of California at Los Angeles.

Ken displays a heart of compassion in an entertainment industry that all too often fosters a self-centered attitude. Ken was the creator and the organizer of the "We are the World" African relief effort. Not only did he arrange the 45 artists who performed the song, but more significantly, Ken created the organiza- tion which supervised the raising and distribution of the funds. Ken similarly cre- ated the "Hands across America" project to raise money for America's hungry. He rallied some seven million Americans to stand hand in hand from the Atlantic to the Pacific. Combined, these two projects have raised $101 million for programs to help society's disadvantaged.

To recognize his efforts, Ken has two rooms full of awards and plaques, including the highly coveted United Nations Peace Medal. Ken Kragen realizes that the glory is not in never failing, but in rising every time you fail.

1112 N. SHERBOURNE DRIVE
LOS ANGELES, CA 90069
(310) 854-4400
FAX (310) 854-0238

Personal Management and
Television Production

Mr. Andy Andrews
P.O. Box 2761
Gulf Shores, AL 36547

Dear Andy;

Thanks for asking me to participate in "Storms of Perfection." I
am honored to be included.

As I try to tell everyone I come in contact with through my
business dealings, lectures and books, "everything in life is an
opportunity - even the negatives." This is a philosophy I've lived
by throughout my entire life. It was taught to me, I'm sure, by my
parents. As a result, I've had very few real setbacks in my life
and have taken even the most difficult situations - the death of a
loved one, the loss of a major client, an injury or illness - and
immediately sought to make something positive of it.

For example, in 1981 my client Harry Chapin was killed in an auto
accident. I reacted to this tragic news by going to work
immediately to raise funds in his memory to continue the work on
the issues of hunger and homelessness which Harry cared so deeply
about. I knew that the window of opportunity to raise significant
dollars was a very small one before people were confronted by some
other event in their lives that would take the edge off their
willingness to give.

I also convinced Kenny Rogers to pick up the torch that had fallen
with Harry and carry it forward, becoming a major champion of these
issues. When in the mid-80s "We Are The World" and "Hands Across
America" rolled around, I felt Harry's loss the most, knowing he
would have been at the forefront of those efforts. Still, I had an
eerie experience one day in New York city, when I actually felt
Harry had somehow crawled up inside me and was directing my
efforts.

Later in the same decade when my mother passed away, many people
remarked to me about what a tragedy it was to lose her. My
response was that it is a tragedy when an eight year old child is

135

killed by a stray bullet. When a 76 year old woman who had lived a wonderful life dies with a minimum of pain and discomfort at a time when her family has had ample time to express their love for her, I look on it rather as a life fulfilled, part of the natural order of things. This is not to say that I do not miss my mother and think about her often, but I try to use those memories in positive ways.

Forty years in the entertainment business have also taught me to take a philosophical approach to lost business. Whenever a client has left me, for example, my first reaction is frankly that it is their loss and not mine. I start thinking about how I won't have to deal with the problems I was having with that client or how I'll have a lot more time to spend with my family. I even wonder what's out there that will be coming my way next. I simply have this undying belief that the future will work itself out; that whatever comes next will be even better and more exciting. I have enough confidence in my own abilities to be secure about the future.

Another setback that we all have to face is illness or injury. I badly injured my neck and was in a brace at the time I began to organize "We Are The World." Later on I realized that the injury had greatly restricted the amount of outside activities I could participate in (particularly basketball, which I love and play frequently). It allowed me to focus completely on the effort of organizing the artists to sing the great song that Lionel Richie and Michael Jackson were in the process of writing.

I used another serious injury and the resulting double spinal fusion as motivation to keep playing full court basketball well into my late '50s. It was a very famous orthopedic surgeon who unwittingly motivated me to keep active. He examined me for some paralysis I was having in one of my legs and informed me that I was lucky to be walking, that I should restrict my activities and be grateful for whatever mobility I had. His negative approach so angered me that I strengthened my back and overcame the problem.

So, Andy, I hope you and everyone who reads your books will remember that everything in life happens for a good reason and that if you can train yourself to believe that, things really do seem to work out for the best,

Sincerely yours,

Ken Kragen

kk/ajs

*"All things are difficult
before they are easy."*

Thomas Fuller

STAN LEE

ILLUSTRATOR/ ENTREPRENEUR

...is Chairman of Marvel Comics and Marvel Films. Stan is the creator of Spider-Man, The Incredible Hulk and hundreds of other comic book heroes.

As the Chairman of Marvel Comics and Marvel Films, Stan Lee is perhaps the most influential personality in the Comic Book industry. He created the superheros which propelled Marvel to its preeminent position. Hundreds of legendary characters such as Spider-Man, The Incredible Hulk, The X-Men, The Fantastic Four, Thor and Dr. Strange all grew out of his fertile imagination.

For years, these comics have given us entertainment and a slice of Americana all their own. Many of these issues are now valuable collectors items.

Stan is also the chairman of the American Spirit Foundation. He has demonstrated an unprecedented ability to communicate with young people through his comics. Stan invites leading members of the entertainment community to join his "Entertainers for Education" committee to make substantive contributions to solving America's education crisis.

MARVEL FILMS
1440 S. SEPULVEDA BLVD., SUITE 114
LOS ANGELES, CALIFORNIA 90025
(310) 444-8638 • FAX: (310) 444-8636

STAN LEE
CHAIRMAN OF THE BOARD

Mr. Andy Andrews
P.O. Box 2761
Gulf Shores, AL 36547

Hi, Andy,

I've rarely followed anyone else's advice in my lifetime, so I
don't know why your readers would want to follow mine. But, for
what it's worth, here's a thought you might want to play with...

You neither learn nor grow by your successes, only by your
failures.

Take me, for example. I wasn't asked to be included in the first
volumes of STORMS OF PERFECTION. So here I am, obviously an
afterthought, a failure in the process of first selection-- but a
better human being because of it.

Failure is the grease that keeps the world's engines running.
It's the adrenaline that sparks the human condition, that keeps
us grasping and groping and growing. But, you have to know how
to deal with failure-- and, most importantly, how to free
yourself of its yoke.

Case in point...

For the first twenty years of my career in comicbooks, I tried in
vain to sell a comicstrip to the major newspaper syndicates. I
wanted to be right up there with the guys who created Dick Tracy,
Terry and the Pirates and Flash Gordon. But, for that entire
twenty-year period, I received rejection after rejection. Talk
about failure-- I was its poster boy!

Did I quit? Did I figure I was wasting my time? Did I give up?
Damn right I did!

I then devoted all my energies to making my comicbooks as good as
they could be. And what happened? After I stopped wasting time

collecting rejection strips from newspaper syndicates and started concentrating on what I did best, Spider-Man, the Incredible Hulk and all our other Marvel heroes made it big, they became world famous.

And then it happened!

The syndicates came after *me*! No more writing countless letters or endlessly knocking on doors-- now I could pick and choose which syndicate I deigned to allow to represent me!

That taught me an unforgetable lesson. I'm just sorry it took me twenty years to learn it.

Persistence is a great virtue. Whatever it is you're trying to accomplish, you should never give up while there's a shred of hope left. *But...*

You must also be perceptive enough to know when something just isn't going to work. There has to be a time when you let it go and look for other opportunities-- the world is filled with them.

Not everybody makes it in every endeavor. Not everybody gets to grab the gold ring in a chosen field. Just as it's important not to give up so long as you have a fighting chance, it's equally important to know when to stop wasting time trying for an impossible goal. It's sometimes better to switch gears, change your direction, find another challenge, one which has a better chance of success.

The trick is not to get hooked on failure. You don't need that monkey on your back. If something doesn't work, jump off the track, take another train. There's a big, wide world out there; you've got countless options-- don't neglect a single one!

Just like me. I suddenly realize that this letter may not be making it, so I'm smart enough to quit-- right now!

All the best,

Stan Lee

"To win without risk is to overcome without glory."

Pierre Corneille

DAVID W. JOHNSON

BUSINESSMAN

...is Chairman, President and Chief Executive Officer of the Campbell Soup Company. Formerly the CEO of Gerber Products company.

David Johnson is responsible for Campbell's Soup's tremendous success since the late 1980's. An Australian native, it was always David's dream to live and work here in America. Although he met with great success in international markets, his dream of coming to America eluded him for many years. He began to wonder if this dream would ever become a reality.

David's business talents were eventually rewarded with an assignment in America. But when did David capture that dream for himself? Was it when he accepted that assignment to work in America? Or, was it when he was giving 110% of his own efforts while assigned to the places he would rather not have been - revealing the qualities in himself that would be so coveted by those giving the assignments in America? Success always occurs when opportunity meets preparedness.

David is now a member of the Board of Colgate-Palmolive Company. He is married to the former Sylvia Raymonde Wells. They live in suburban Philadelphia and have three grown sons.

Campbell SOUP *Company*

WORLD HEADQUARTERS
Camden, New Jersey 08103-1799

DAVID W. JOHNSON
CHAIRMAN, PRESIDENT AND
CHIEF EXECUTIVE OFFICER

Dear Andy:

Even though I was born in the snowy mountains of Australia, I enjoy telling people that Chicago is my home town. That's because Chicago was my first experience of the United States and the beginning of a love affair that has lasted a lifetime.

When I graduated from the University of Chicago, a number of leading U.S. companies offered me a job. I couldn't accept, as my student visa was conditioned on a return to my home country. "Don't worry," I said to myself, "in a few years they will be begging you to return...." Famous last words!

In Australia, I joined Colgate Palmolive as a management trainee and indicated my strong preference to follow an International career. I never doubted that my business journey would bring me back to a world headquarters in the U.S.A.

Promotion followed promotion and I was moved to Africa. However, I was very aware that Australia and Africa were remote outreaches of corporate empire. After six years in Africa I asked my boss (the President of International) where my next move might take me. He said greater responsibility in Africa and most likely including the Middle East. Hardly the answer I wanted. I queried, "Why not Europe and then challenge in the U.S.?" He said simply, "because you are a third country national and we can make the greatest gains using your talent and pioneer spirit in emerging countries."

Those words should have inspired me but they didn't. Instead, I read them as a kind of sentence to serve forever in an elite, but foreign legion. Those "few years" I had envisioned in Chicago now looked to be stretching into decades. I knew and understood the importance of earning one's spurs in international markets, but was I to be marooned? Would bells toll, but not for me?

I had been trained at one of the great business schools of the world and I wanted to grow and be ready to solve the toughest problems a global business could face. What now?

Doubt began to intrude. My once-clear path was dimming. My dream of America and world business leadership was receding.

I was forced to make a very tough decision. One that was against my instincts and feelings. That was to leave a wonderful company and search to reshape a future that would take me on a new growth path. Adieu, Colgate and Africa.

I next joined Warner Lambert Company. I moved to Hong Kong and had responsibility for Asia. This region stretched from Philippines to Pakistan, from Japan to New Zealand. My key role was to integrate and build the newly acquired Parke Davis businesses into Warner Lambert. The work was exciting and stretching. Married with three young children, I threw myself into the job. Travel in the region found me away from home over 50% of the time. It was tough on our family. The business grew lustily. Two years passed. Then three.

At the beginning of the fourth year, the Company's C.E.O. came on a visit and my wife said, "If you get a chance, are you going to ask what might be the next assignment?" I said, "I think I better keep quiet and hope that my track record of results will speak for me." Presentations and field trips were part of a crash program of visits. I proudly described progress in Japan as a highlight.

At the end of his visit, as we drove to Hong Kong's Kai Tak airport, the big boss asked "Have you ever considered coming into the U.S. to work?" I could have fainted! You can guess what I said. And he did invite me. And the rest is history with an exciting fulfillment of my brightest dreams. And one of the best outcomes was again to serve Colgate-Palmolive; this time as a Director.

Seizing the Future . . . .

Your friend,

David

*"The time to repair the roof
is when the sun is shining."*

John F. Kennedy

FRANK E. PERETTI

AUTHOR

...is a Christian novelist who has over 5 million books in print. Articles featuring Frank have appeared in USA Today, People, The LA Times, *and many other publications.*

Articles about Frank Peretti and his books have appeared in *USA Today, People, The Saturday Evening Post, The Los Angeles Times* and many other publications. He is a natural storyteller who, as a youngster in Seattle, regularly gathered the neighborhood children for animated story-telling sessions.

As an adult, Frank spent time studying English, screen writing and film at UCLA. After college he assisted his father in pastoring a small church in Vashon Island, Washington.

Frank's success as an author has been phenomenal. The two novels of spiritual warfare, *This Present Darkness* (1988) and *Piercing the Darkness* (1989), have captivated readers, together selling more than 3.5 million copies. The total number of books in print for all of his adult and children's books is more than 5.2 million.

```
                    Frank E. Peretti
                  Blanton-Harrell, Inc.
                    2910 Poston Avenue
                 Nashville, Tennessee  37203


Mr. Andy Andrews
P.O. Box 2761
Gulf Shores, Alabama  36547

Dear Andy:

The Bible says the whole reason for trials and struggles is
to refine us, make us strong, and increase our faith.  Well,
looking back over the past three decades, that's how it was
with me.

Sure, God made me to be a writer, and since I was a child,
that was my dream.  I spent hours up in my room writing and
drawing comics; I gathered the neighborhood kids under the
back porch and told them stories; I never missed
"Disneyland" on television and dreamed of being like Walt
Disney.

But what a long journey it was between the dream and the
reality!  All through my early adult years, the writing
never worked out.  I tried to write stories for magazines
and ended up collecting rejection letters.  I tried writing
for television and ... well, would you believe I got
rejected for being "too innovative?"  As for being a
novelist, I either didn't have the time or couldn't get the
ideas.

So, I spent many years wandering from one profession to
another:  McDonald's french fry flunkie (I got fired the
second day), shipscaler, musician in studios and musician on
the road,  printer (fired again), carpenter, ski factory
worker, and finally college student.  After all that, I
decided to go into the ministry and help my Dad pastor a
small rural church.

The pastoral ministry didn't work out either.  At the end of
five years, I was burned out, at the end of my rope, washed
up, and no closer to my dream than before, or so I thought.
I was thirty-two, my wife and I were living in a twenty-four
foot travel trailer with a shack built around it, we were
```

poor and in debt and I didn't know what in the world I was
going to do with myself. I'd already tried most everything
I thought I wanted to do, but now here I sat, unsuccessful
at all of them.

Being a religious man, I prayed a lot for guidance and
direction, but whenever I prayed, the only answer I got from
the Lord was, "Write the Book." I had come up with an idea
for a full-length novel a few years earlier while pounding
nails as a carpenter; I'd actually started the project and
given it up several times while pastoring the church; I'd
never had anything published before, not even a short story;
I'd already queried fourteen different publishers and been
turned down or ignored by every one of them.

But when God makes you a writer and tells you to write,
that's what you do, so in between odd jobs to help put food
on the table, I dug out that ragged old novel and started
tinkering and scribbling away at it once again. What I
finally ended up with was a manuscript of over seven hundred
typewritten pages - and no money.

So I came full circle: I went back to the ski factory where
I'd worked years before and started all over again, doing
the same menial job I did the first time, and feeling like
I'd not gone one step forward in my life.

But you see, this was all in God's timing; it was all His
plan. Frank Peretti still had some willfulness,
selfishness, and pride that had to be weeded out of his
life, and it took two more years in the ski factory to get
that accomplished. Like Jesus said, "For everyone to whom
much is given, from him much will be required."

In God's own timing, *This Present Darkness* was finally
published in 1986, became a bestseller in 1988, and has
remained on the Christian bestseller list ever since, along
with its sequel, *Piercing the Darkness*, and two other
novels, *Prophet* and *The Oath*. The books have inspired and
encouraged millions of readers in over fourteen different
languages, and, I understand, helped to establish fiction as
a viable and marketable field in Christian publishing.

In my office, I still have a snow ski from the factory,
signed by all the friends I made while working there and

given to me as a memento on my last day. I keep it to remember the years of struggle, the lessons learned, and the faithfulness of God's calling on my life.

In the front of *This Present Darkness* is a dedication I made to my wife Barbara:

> To Barbara Jean, wife and friend,
> who loved me and waited.

Through all the years of struggling and wandering, she never gave up on me, never stopped loving me, and always waited in faith, knowing God had a plan.

And I guess He did, didn't He?

Sometimes it's good to look back just to see how far we've come, how much we've grown, and how faithful God can be.

Thanks for the opportunity to do just that.

God bless,

Frank E. Peretti

Frank E. Peretti

MORRIS HACKNEY

BUSINESSMAN

...is Chairman and Chief Executive Officer of the Citation Corporation, one of the largest companies in the iron casting industry.

Morris Hackney is chairman and CEO of Citation Corporation, which he founded 20 years ago as a small company. Today Citation Corporation has grown to eight divisions in six states and sales of more than 300 million annually. Since 1980, the company sales have grown at a compounded 25% rate annually. The shares of common stock, which went public at $8 dollars a share last year have increased more that 62% in less that eight months.

Citation Corporation has grown from a single location producer of ductile iron castings to one of the largest companies in the casting industry. Today, the company produces castings in gray and ductile iron, steel and aluminum for a wide variety of industries in the United States, Mexico and Canada. The corporation has grown to approximately 3,000 employees. Morris was president and CEO of the Hackney Corporation prior to founding Citation Corporation. He is a 1949 graduate of the United States Naval Academy.

CITATION

CITATION CORPORATION

2 Office Park Circle
Suite 204
Birmingham, AL 35223
(205) 871-5731
FAX (205) 870-8211

Mr. Andy Andrews
P.O. Box 2761
Gulf Shores, Alabama 36547

Dear Andy,

Something that I have realized over the course of my business career is that everyone's life has the same amount of luck. The difference is some take advantage of it and others don't. I believe the reason for this is that luck is sometimes disguised or camouflaged as an insignificant or even disastrous event! Let me give you an example:

After returning home from the service I went to work for my father as 10% owner of a modest hardware store. Over the next 15 or 16 years we transformed the store into a chain link fence business that ultimately expanded into a $35 million company. My father was approaching retirement age by then so my brothers and I decided it would be best to sell. We executed a successful sale and, in the agreement, I remained on staff in a management capacity. Then, at 42 years of age, I was fired. Literally on the street at a time of life that one shouldn't be thinking about starting over.

At the time it seemed disastrous. Add to this the fact that I had leveraged the proceeds of the chain link fence business sale to buy a small foundry that was failing, and it seemed doubly disastrous. We had done business with this particular foundry previously so I thought I knew the business. It turned out I didn't. I struggled with it for two and half years. Every month losing more and more money with one piece of bad news after another. There were many times during this process that I wanted to quit. In fact, I would have if I'd had an alternative. I even tried to sell a number of times but the business was doing so poorly no one would buy it. I learned many lessons about business in those years and, out of an apparent disastrous period of my life, came a shining success. We finally assembled the right management team, we learned how to run the foundry efficiently and things took an upturn.

Today my interest in the foundry business is worth $100 million. Please don't take that as a boastful statement. It simply represents the result of doing your best everyday...learning and applying what you've learned everyday in the process of becoming successful. I took the lessons learned in turning that business around and started another company specializing in buying struggling businesses and "fixing" them, making them profitable and then selling them. My interest in this business, The Hackney Group, is roughly $25 million.

I tell you this, Andy, only to make the point that I thought being fired at 42 was a disaster at the time. Had I continued working at the chain link fence company I would be nearing retirement today at about $50,000 annually. The fact that I was fired led me (or perhaps pressured me) to be a part of the success my companies now enjoy. So disaster was actually camouflaged luck! Life deals all of us strange hands at times. It's important to remember that the game isn't over until we say it is. Doing your best everyday, learning and applying what you learn will create long term success every time. Thank you for the opportunity to share my experiences with you and your readers, Andy. I wish you continued success in your journey.

Sincerely,

T. Morris Hackney

Morris Hackney

MANUEL

CUSTOM CLOTHING DESIGNER

...sewing since the age of seven, Manuel has designed custom clothes for many people from Ronald Reagan to James Dean.

Manuel's first name is his trademark. His name is synonymous with the successful, glamorous look of the stars. Manuel is the man who put Elvis in a jumpsuit. He made Johnny Cash the "Man in Black." He is the custom fashion designer who has decked out politicians, entertainers and the most notable stars of society. Manuel is the "Cowboy Couture" and "The couturier of Rock 'n Roll." Country Music entertainer Terry McBride says, "Getting a first Manuel jacket is a rite of passage for an artist."

Manuel was born in Mexico, and was put into the work force at the tender age of twelve. He had been sewing since the age of seven. So, when he began working for a tailor shop in his pre-teen years, he had already developed an aptitude for his profession. He had also already formed his dream of beings an artist with clothing.

Manuel points out that even success can bring the dark clouds of a storm. It is not an easy thing to turn your back on what most would call success in order to follow your dream of attaining something even better. Manuel took a risk and clutched his dream with a death grip, forsaking all options of settling for anything less. For Manuel, and his hundreds of fanatically loyal clientele, it has made all the difference.

manuel

Andy Andrews
P.O. Box 2761
Gulf Shores, Alabama 36547

Dear Andy,

My dream to become a designer of personal image, not just clothes, started when I was seven or eight years old. I noticed that much of the way we looked and dressed was pre-set by society and that we all more or less dressed like soldiers in the same uniform. This was particularly true for males. I never believed that it should be this way. We are all individuals with special gifts, looks, talents and personalitites that can be brought to the front by understanding and design. I found that I could do this well. I suppose this was *my* particular talent. The creative side and the communication between my clients / friends has always been fun for me.

The challenges for me came not from the creative / design side but the financial / business side. Finding the right combination of people to work and communicate with for my staff and finding the money to keep us all alive at payroll time! This was an ongoing struggle for me for a long, long time.

Then, a new kind of challenge came dressed in the camouflage of apparent success. Large design houses came to me offering to buy my designs and set me up in entire *Manuel* sections of the largest, finest department stores across the country. This represents lots of money and success in America... but was it what I wanted? Was it true to the dream that started growing in me as a young boy? After struggling for so long with money here was a way to end that struggle - offered to me on a silver platter! I had to consider my options. And I had to consider my creative soul. In short, I had to *focus*. I had to focus on my goals, my dreams and what I wanted my name to mean in the future.

I declined the generous offers of the design houses. They did not represent what I represent. You cannot buy a one of a kind work of art, designed specifically for the personality who wears it, off the rack. I decided to continue pursuing my dream with this renewed focus and have since designed for and built wonderful friendships with many of the world's most successful entertainers, business people and politicians.

So, you see Andy, as strange as it may sound, my dream could have been stolen by "success." *Focus* on my true purpose led Manuel to the prize with which I am now very happy and comfortable.

Sincerely,

Manuel

Manuel

1922 Broadway • Nashville, Tennessee 37203 • (615) 321-5444 Fax (615) 321-5658

JOHN MOSCHITTA, JR.

ACTOR

...is listed in the 1995 Guinness Book *for speaking 586 words per minute. He can be seen on "Sesame Street," "Saved By The Bell" and many television commercials.*

Who can forget those famous Federal Express TV commercials? John Moschitta has been listed in the Guinness book of world records for speaking 586 words per minute! He says that growing up in a family of 5 sisters forced him to talk fast just to get a word in edgewise. As a teenager, John struggled in his pursuit of an entertainment career. He supplemented his income by working in a mental health clinic and as a fast food clown (until he was robbed at knife point; prompting him to put the clown suit away).

John appeared in a variety of TV shows until he landed the "commercial of the decade." The fast paced world of Federal Express was exemplified by John's light-speed lips. Since then, his phone hasn't stopped ringing. He has appeared in person or voice in numerous TV shows, movies, cartoons and of course TV commercials.

John gives generously of himself in his association with the "Starlight Foundation," a non-profit organization dedicated to enhancing the lives of seriously ill children.

DEAR ANDY,

IT'S A GREAT HONOR TO BE INCLUDED IN YOUR "STORMS OF PERFECTION" SERIES.

I LEARNED WHAT I CONSIDER TO BE ONE OF MY MOST IMPORTANT LIFE LESSONS WHILE
I WAS A STARVING ACTOR IN NEW YORK WORKING AS A RECEPTIONIST AT A MENTAL
HEALTH CLINIC. SO MANY OF THE PATIENTS HAD WHAT, BY ANY STANDARDS, WOULD
BE CONSIDERED OVERWHELMING PROBLEMS. YET IN THE FACE OF ALL THEIR
ADVERSITY THEY LED VERY NORMAL PRODUCTIVE LIVES. ON THE OTHER HAND THERE
WERE PATIENTS WHO REQUIRED HOSPITALIZATION OVER A HANG NAIL. I LEARNED
THEN AND THERE, IT WASN'T THE MAGNITUDE OF YOUR PROBLEMS BUT THE WAY YOU
ALLOW THEM TO EFFECT YOU THAT MATTERS IN LIFE. EVERYTHING IS RELATIVE.
ACCEPT RESPONSIBILITY FOR YOUR LIFE, BE TRUE TO YOURSELF AND DON'T SWEAT THE
ROADBLOCKS YOU CAN'T CONTROL.

CERTAINLY OVER THE YEARS THERE HAVE BEEN MANY ROADBLOCKS. A FEW YEARS
AGO I ENCOUNTERED WHAT WAS FOR ME A MAJOR ROADBLOCK. IT'S THE OLD
HOLLYWOOD STORY; MISAPPROPRIATION OF FUNDS BY A TRUSTED FINANCIAL
MANAGER. I AWOKE ONE MORNING TO FIND THAT MY SAVINGS WERE DEPLETED, A
SECOND AND THIRD MORTGAGE HAD BEEN TAKEN OUT ON MY HOUSE AND I HAD IN
EXCESS OF $70,000 IN UNPAID BILLS. ON TOP OF THAT, THE RECESSION WAS IN FULL
BLOOM AND MY WORK LOAD HAD DECREASED 70%. WELL I WAS DEVASTATED.

DESPITE SUGGESTIONS BY SEVERAL LAWYERS TO DECLARE BANKRUPTCY, I DECIDED TO
FACE UP TO MY RESPONSIBILITY AND RIGHT THE WRONGS. ALTHOUGH I WASN'T THE
ONE WHO TOOK THE MONEY, I WAS THE ONE WHO ALLOWED IT TO HAPPEN. FOR THE
PAST THREE YEARS IT HAS BEEN A VERY SLOW UPHILL BATTLE TO ONCE AGAIN GAIN
CONTROL OF MY LIFE. THERE WERE MANY TIMES ALONG THE WAY I WANTED TO GIVE
UP BUT MY FAITH IN MYSELF AND MY BELIEF THAT BY DOING THE RIGHT THING I
WOULD EVENTUALLY TRIUMPH KEPT ME GOING. ON MANY OCCASIONS EVEN MY
FRIENDS ENCOURAGED ME TO THROW IN THE TOWEL BUT I JUST COULDN'T.

I AM HAPPY TO REPORT THAT THERE IS NOW A LIGHT AT THE END OF THE TUNNEL. I CAN
ANTICIPATE A TIME IN THE VERY NEAR FUTURE WHEN I CAN CLOSE THIS CHAPTER IN
MY LIFE AND MOVE ON TO THINGS THAT ARE MORE IMPORTANT TO ME.

SOME PEOPLE THINK I WAS FOOLISH TO STRUGGLE FOR THE PAST FEW YEARS. I DO NOT.
I HAVE RISEN FROM THE ASHES A STRONGER , WISER AND HOPEFULLY BETTER PERSON.
AND I HAVE DONE SO WITHOUT SACRIFICING THOSE THINGS WHICH ARE MOST
IMPORTANT TO ME .... MY FAMILY, FRIENDS AND MY POSITIVE ATTITUDE.

I FULLY EXPECT THERE TO BE MANY MORE ROADBLOCKS IN MY LIFE BUT I KNOW I'LL
HAVE THE STRENGTH TO PERSEVERE AND ABOVE ALL REMAIN TRUE TO MYSELF AND BE
HAPPY. IT'S NOT THE HAND YOU'RE DEALT ... IT'S THE WAY YOU PLAY THE CARDS !

MY BEST,

John Moschitta, Jr.

956 Chattanooga Avenue, Pacific Palisades, California 90272

ANDREA JAEGER

FORMER PROFESSIONAL TENNIS PLAYER

...at 14 years of age she became the second youngest player to ever win a pro tennis tournament. Now retired, she holds 14 WTA Tour singles titles.

Andrea Jaeger knows the pain of emotional isolation. At Wimbledon in 1983, she found success very quickly. She soon found that she was too famous to make friends at high school and too young to find close friends on the pro tennis circuit. Andrea rebelled against her reputation as a wonder kid. She found herself very unhappy. Then, three years after turning pro, Andrea's lightning ascent ended with a shoulder injury. The injury finally caused the end of her pro tennis career in 1987.

Eager to be productive, Andrea (whose seven-figure winnings were kept in trust accounts) took a $6.00 an hour job as a switchboard operator. She then sustained major injuries when a drunk driver collided with her car. While still enduring the pain of her tennis injury, in addition to her other serious injuries she received in the auto collision, Andrea managed to lay the framework for her "Kid's Stuff Foundation." Feeling as though she had been robbed of her own childhood, Andrea's heart warmed to children suffering life-threatening diseases. Andrea's "Silver Lining Ranch" for children is well named and reveals the attitude that earned her the 1994 "Player Who Makes a Difference" award, which was created by *Family Circle* magazine to honor players who make the most outstanding contribution of time and energy to worth while causes.

**The Silver
Lining Ranch**
Kids' Stuff Foundation, Inc.

Andy Andrews
P.O. Box 2761
Gulf Shores, Alabama 36547

Dear Andy,

Wow. Discussing one of my biggest disappointments certainly brings up the memories. I was a professional tennis player at age fourteen. I played against and beat such players as Martina Navratilova, Chris Evert and Billie Jean King. My highest ranking was number two in the world! I made it to the finals of Wimbledon one year. At age eighteen I went to hit a backhand and my shoulder popped. I defaulted that match and three months later I was sitting in the Olympic athletes dorm crying because I would have to pull out of the Olympic competition. Letting down my country, my family, friends and myself was not a fun experience. I have had seven shoulder surgeries since that time in an effort to correct the problem. I may have been one of the youngest to be on the professional circuit and I suppose I was also one of the youngest to have to leave it forever. Those events took a lot of strength to get through but they were not part of my biggest disappointment.

After I left the tennis circuit I started up Kids' Stuff Foundation, a non- profit organization that provides opportunities for children with cancer and other life threatening diseases. I started it with my own money and a friend of mine, John McEnroe, donated to help the program reach as many children as possible. Raising money and non-profit work is much more difficult than anything I ever did on the tennis court. In tennis I practiced hard and was in control of my own results when I was on court. With the foundation I was finding that even if you worked twelve hours a day and did everything possible, it did not guarantee a donation from someone.

After working the major part of a year we were close to finalizing a large donation from a national corporation. I talked to the representatives and we had actually gotten to the point of scheduling a press conference to announce the donation. I was beyond excited. This grant would allow the foundation to continue it's efforts for an entire year. It could not have come at a better time as we were desperate for funding.

P.O. BOX 10970   ASPEN, COLORADO 81612   303·925·9540   FAX 303·544·0565

The time came for the announcement and no one called. I called the company and got the run around for a month. Finally, after four weeks of sweating it out I talked to the representative who so brilliantly avoided me. "I am sorry, Miss Jaeger, I do not see your name on the donation list."

"Are you sure?" I can hear her go over page after page and yet no sign of Andrea Jaeger or Kids' Stuff Foundation on her list.

"Yes, I am positive." Then I hear a click and the line is dead. I couldn't even hang up the phone. Tears welled up in my eyes and my heart sank. All the children I was getting to know a hospitals around the country would now have to suffer more. I went straight to my room and laid in bed for two days, severely disappointed. It was one of the few times in my life I have ever done that. In fact, I think it was the only time. Rejection is never easy to handle, but that situation just tore everything up inside of me.

The sun kept coming up and on the third day I sprang out of bed thinking - this will not end the foundation. That was over five years ago and even though we still struggle to get donations, Kids' Stuff has continued to bring smiles to sick children's faces and laughter to their hearts.

I am glad I have never given up on anything. If you have the will in your mind and your heart, I really believe you can accomplish anything. It may not be the path you predicted, but rainbows can shine through your efforts.

Sincerely,

Andrea Jaeger

158

*"Let our advance worrying
become advance thinking
and planning."*

Winston Churchill

NORMAN E. MILLER

BUSINESSMAN

...is Chairman of Interstate Battery System of America. Interstate has become the number one replacement battery brand in North America.

Norm Miller is an American entrepreneur who has developed a multi-million dollar auto battery business while believing that religion not only belongs in the workplace, but is an essential part of business success. Norm's unorthodox approach to business, which includes company sponsored Bible studies and prayer groups for employees, has been a tremendous success. It does, however, occasionally generate ridicule from a secular business market that does not understand Norm's success or his heart. This, however; is not the painful issue Norm chose to depict as his "Storm of Perfection." Rather, his storm came before his taking the helm of his corporation.

It is always the pioneers who get the arrows shot at them. The nail that stands the tallest is the one which receives the first blows of the hammer. Norm Miller is a man of convictions pointing America's compass back toward its earlier values and former glory. He has my respect and admiration for doing so.

Andy Andrews
P.O. Box 2761
Gulf Shores, Alabama 36547

Dear Andy:

To be asked to contribute to a book of this nature is an honor I do not regard lightly. I am convinced that more is learned from our difficult experiences and what might be perceived as failure, than from whatever achievements and successes have come our way. For sure this has been true in my case. I lived a troubled life for many years and I'd like to share with your readers how I came from where I was to where I am, by God's grace, today.

I grew up in Galveston, Texas, where my dad ran a service station and garage, so I've been around cars for as long as I can remember. That's probably why I ended up in the battery business. But I inherited something else from my dad -- drinking. I followed in my dad's footsteps and started drinking in junior high school. For more years than I care to admit, my major game plan was to have fun and party.

Somehow I made it to college where I drank and partied even more. I wasn't much of a student, but managed to complete college and marry Anne, the girl of my dreams. That year my dad started an Interstate Battery distributorship and Anne and I moved to Memphis where I worked with him and my brothers. Later, I moved to Dallas where I began working directly for Interstate in the national office. That meant I was on the road a lot, traveling across the country selling and setting up distributorships. Drinking, partying, and selling batteries -- that pretty much defined my life-style at that time. The drinking seemed to ease a pressure that built up in me every four or five days.

After several years, my wife had decided that sooner or later she was going to leave me. I'd been drinking for twenty years, and the tension this created in our marriage forced her into that decision. By now we had two children. I was doing great with Interstate, but behind the scene at home there were some problems. One night back in 1974, I ended up drinking as usual until the bars closed, but afterward, as I was driving home, I got pulled over by the police. I talked my way out of getting arrested. However, the next morning all hung over, I called in sick to work. As I lay there in bed, the truth overwhelmed me. I was an alcoholic! I'd lost control of my life. That was a frightening realization! In that instant of desperation and realization, panic hit me. Terrified, I blurted out in a half-yell, "God help me! I can't handle it!" I realize it doesn't happen that way for everyone, but God took the compulsion to drink away completely. If you had asked me the day before if I believed in God, I would have told you that I didn't know, that I hadn't even really thought about it.

INTERSTATE BATTERY SYSTEM OF AMERICA, INC.
12770 Merit Drive • Suite 400 • Dallas, Texas 75251 • (214) 991-1444 • FAX 458-8288

Religion meant nothing to me and I seldom went to church, but about this same time, a friend started telling me what the Bible says about life and living it. I quickly cut him off. "If you can show me how I can accept the Bible as the TRUTH, logically with my brain, then I'll pay attention to what it has to say. Otherwise, as far as I'm concerned, it's just another old book, a bunch of people's outdated philosophies or whatever, and I don't need it."

I thought I was throwing my friend a big challenge, but he met me head on and gave me some books which documented the validity of the claim that the Bible is God's truth. I was overwhelmed by the objective evidence concerning the Bible from three major areas: From archaeological discoveries, the history and weight of manuscript authenticity, and most of all, from the proven fulfillment of Old Testament prophecy hundreds of years later in the New Testament. I studied all this thoroughly and it left no doubt in my mind that the Bible is indeed the Word of God given to man exactly as He intended it.

The supporting evidence was so strong that I began reading the Bible, and my wife and I attended a Bible study class. An important verse from the Bible spoke of the need to seek for truth and that you'd find it (see Matt. 7:11). I told God if He was for real I was a "seeker" and that I wanted to find the TRUTH. So we kept studying the Bible and going to the Bible study. I learned that "Jesus is the Way, the Truth, and the Life" (John 14:6); and that we are all "slaves" (2 Pet. 2:19), not just to alcohol and drugs, bad habits and other things, but overall to *sin*, and that, as a result, our lives fall short of the glory of God (Rom. 3:23). The Bible also showed me that "the Truth shall make you free" (John 8:32), and Christ is the TRUTH! I longed for freedom. I recognized that my life-style wasn't pleasing to God, and that I needed to humble myself, change my mind about preconceived ideas about God, Jesus and the Bible, and trust Jesus for forgiveness and the ability to live life God's way. I made a decision about Christ's claims and my life hasn't been the same!

Many things have happened in my life since I made that decision -- fear went out of my life and love came in and daily I experience the fullness of life God intended for us. All of what has happened in my life -- the good stuff and the less-than-good things -- have brought me to the understanding that God loves us, we are His created offspring, He is our heavenly Father, and my career, popularity, or the success of my personal relationships and Interstate Batteries, will be measured on how I use my life loving Him and loving and serving others.

At Interstate we make the claim that our batteries are "built to last," and we stand back of our claims. Regardless how good a battery may be, it won't last forever, but the greatest thing that ever happened to me was when I became charged for life with the truth that sets people free here now and forever more!

Sincerely,

Norm Miller

162

*"There is no substitution
for guts."*

Paul "Bear" Bryant

MERLIN OLSEN

ACTOR/BROADCASTER

...is quickly recognized as "Jonathan Garvey" from "Little House on the Prairie" and the FTD "Flower Man." This former NFL athlete is now a member of the Children's Miracle Network Board of Directors.

For years, Merlin Olsen was watched with anxiety and dread by opponents who waited for him to cross the line of scrimmage; nervously anticipating the center's snap and the onslaught of the Los Angeles Ram's Fearsome Foursome. He has conversely been viewed with delight by children and adults alike as he entertained us with his acting ability on such famed television series as "Little House on the Prairie," "Father Murphy" and others. The flavor he brought to a football game as a sportscaster quickly earned him top honors at CBS and NBC television networks.

Merlin Olsen has reached success in an unusually wide breadth of endeavors. He became a member of the Pro Football Hall of Fame after an exciting 15 year career in the NFL, during which he displayed his aggressive determination to win. At the same time, Merlin is recognized as "The Flower Man" - a spokesman for FTD Florists. He also holds a masters degree in economics and is a motivational speaker who relates to people everywhere that they can attain their greatest hopes so long as they never lose sight of their dream.

Most of us see Merlin Olsen as a gentle giant. He has contributed to countless charitable efforts an works diligently to raise funds for the Children's Miracle Network. Merlin recognizes that our children are the keepers of our best hopes and greatest fears. Merlin himself was confronted during childhood with the decision of whether to quit or drive on with his dreams. No one can doubt he made the right choice.

Merlin Olsen

Mr. Andy Andrews
P.O. Box 2761
Gulf Shores, AL 36547

Dear Andy,

I have truly enjoyed the inspiring stories contained in the letters from Storms of Perfection and was delighted to be asked to be a part of the special series. Life is full of challenges which can become even more difficult when obstacles like rejection and adversity are added to the mix. I know because these "Dream Killers" almost overwhelmed me at a very early age.

Where do our early ideas come from: What would cause a young 8 year old boy to respond to his mother's question, "What do you want to do when you grow up?" with, "I want to be big and I want to be an athlete."

My mother quickly explained to me that we don't just decide to be big. She said that with grandmothers 4'11" and 5'1", grandfathers who were both 5'7" and a father that was 5'11"; that growing big was not going to be easy. Being an athlete, however, was a more realistic goal. That was something I could work toward achieving.

As it turned out, it was easier for me to grow than it was to develop my athletic ability. My coordination was so slow in developing that in spite of enthusiastic attempts and determined efforts I had been quickly cut from every team I had tried out for.

At the age of 15, I was in 9th grade and had grown to be about 5'10" and 150 lbs. I was involved in tryouts for the basketball team when the coach, once again, called me into his office to tell me that I was being cut from the team. I can still remember the pain of standing there biting my lip and trying to fight back the tears.

The coach put his hand on my shoulder and said, "Why are you doing this to yourself? Our job here at the junior high school is to develop athletes for high school. You are never going to be an athlete. Why don't you go out for the school play or work on the school paper. Do something where your efforts won't be wasted."

How different my life would have been if I had listened to that 9th grade coach...if I had given up on my dreams.

Less than a year later I finally made the sophomore football team. As I continued to grow and to become more coordinated I went on to make the swimming team, to run track and to play basketball at the high school. But I can still remember vividly the excitement of my first football game. The incredible sense of a dream fulfilled.

Football provided a scholarship for my college education and before long I even dared to dream about playing professional football. Later on there were dreams about being an actor and a broadcaster and yes, those dreams too would be fulfilled.

You can probably understand why I still believe in dreams and their importance in our lives whether we're 8 or 18 or 80. Dreams fuel the fire that burns inside of each of us. A fire that helps us find our way past the obstacles blocking the pathway to success.

Looking back today, I sometimes wonder why I was so stubborn. Why I didn't just give up and walk away. Clinging on to my dreams and believing in myself allowed me to turn these dreams into a reality and to discover that the real life equivalent was even better than the dreams themselves.

Sincerely,

Merlin Olsen

PATTY WETTERLING

CHILDREN'S RIGHTS ADVOCATE

...co-founded the Jacob Wetterling Foundation after her son's abduction. Jacob was 11 on October 22, 1989, when a man abducted him at gunpoint.

When I read Patty Wetterling's letter, I was astounded at the remarkable strength and hope she displays considering the tragedy she continues to endure. I cannot conceive any greater anguish than to be subjected to the abduction of your own child - living with the unanswered questions: "Where is my baby tonight?" and "Will I ever see him again?" and "How can I go on without my child?" What worse pain and anguish could one experience?

Patty was not willing to suffer without action. In her own words, she reveals that "Hope is an action word." Patty now serves as a board member for several organizations, including the Jacob Wetterling Foundation, to assist in the protection of children, and the search for those abducted. Patty exemplifies the greater part of our human spirit as she has taken up a cause and created change on a grand scale.

When I think of Patty Wetterling, I am reminded of the quote: "A hundred years from now, it will not matter what my bank account was, the sort of house I lived in, or the kind of car I drove, but the world may be different because I was important in the life of a child."

Mr. Andy Andrews
P.O. Box 2761
Gulf Shores, Alabama   36547

Dear Andy,

On October 22, 1989, my 11 year old son was kidnapped by a masked gunman while riding his bike home from a convenience store with his best friend and his younger brother. For days and weeks I cried, I yelled, I walked around in a trance supported by friends and family who made me eat, made me go for walks, gave me the strength to do interviews with reporters all across the nation, all in hopes of finding Jacob.

The very nature of having a missing child leaves people feeling helpless, alone, frightened, sad and in many ways paralyzed by all the what ifs?

I remember clearly one day laying in bed pulling the covers over my head and saying, "I can't do this any more. It's too hard. It hurts too much." As I curled up into a ball and rolled over, I had this vision of Jacob doing the same thing, echoing my thoughts with "They're never going to find me. They've given up. I'll never make it home. I can't do this any more."

I found myself immediately holding this conversation with him saying 'Hold on Jacob. Don't give up. We'll find you but you have to keep going until we do. Stay strong. I love you.'

It was at that point I made a decision. I will do anything in my power to find Jacob and other missing children. I will fight until the end to stop this problem from happening to other children, other families. There is so much to do. I know so little. But there is nothing in the world more important to me than my children. I knew then that I had to get up and begin this new journey.

We have circulated millions of Missing posters. We have traveled across the country to raise the awareness of missing children. We made some important legislative changes in Minnesota and then fought for three years in Washington D.C. for federal legislation to help protect children. Finally last year, Congress passed the Jacob Wetterling Crimes Against Children Sex Offender Registration Act as part of the 1994 Crime Bill. I've spoken to thousands of children and adults about abduction prevention and child safety issues. I applaud

P.O. Box 639, 32 1st Avenue NW St. Joseph, MN 56374 612-363-0470 1-800-325-HOPE Fax# 612=363=0473

and smile inside when I hear of an attempted abduction where a child gets away because they knew what to do.

I learned that kids can come home if we don't give up on them. I share stories about how these children are located after 2 years, 7 years, in one case 22 years! I hope and pray for every child that is abducted. I have learned how Hope is an action word and is truly a motivator as to why each of us gets out of bed in the morning. Little Hopes, big Hopes. I've learned how we must decide to move forward and take control over the things we can control in our lives even though there are always going to be things we can't control.

I spoke to a group of fifth graders and one girl raised her hand and said,"My mom says Jacob's dead and you're just wasting your time." All I could say to her was, "What if he's **not**? What if Jacob's still out there waiting to be found and we all look at our watches and calenders and say he's probably not coming home and give up on him, leaving him in whatever situation he's had to be in to survive?" And what about the other 300 children who are abducted every year. I find it hard to believe they're **all** not coming home. Odds are some of them are still alive. As a searching parent, I hope mine is one that will come home. Meanwhile we must all continue raising the awareness for everyone to be watchful.

When Jacob was kidnapped, many things in my life became clear. What matters and what doesn't. I know the value of dreams and never giving up. If we have no vision of what we hope will happen, how can we take the steps to get there?

We need to listen to children. Molly, a second grader wrote this:

"This song is to Jacob and Mom and Dad. It's called I Love You. I love you Jacob but I can't come give you a hug. But there is one thing I can do is find you in my heart, and Love you."

Never give up. Never forget. We are all Jacob's hope. We are the hope for a safe future for all children everywhere. There's much to be done.

Please hold our missing children in your hearts until we can hold them in our arms again.

Thanks for the opportunity to share. Thank you for caring.

Sincerely,

Patty Wetterling

Patty Wetterling
Jacob's mom

"There are many ways to measure success, not the least of which is the way your child describes you when talking to a friend."

Anonymous

SHANNON MILLER

WORLD CHAMPION GYMNAST

...is the most decorated American Gymnast, male or female, in history, having won more Olympic and World Championship medals than any other American gymnast.

Little Shannon Miller won the hearts of Americans everywhere with her inspiring gymnastics performance during the 1992 Olympic games in Barcelona, Spain. Her silver medal performance was the highest all-around finish ever by an American woman at a non-boycotted games. Shannon, America's smallest athlete in the 1992 games, won a total of 5 medals for the USA.

Shannon began her career in gymnastics at the age of 6. At 18 years of age, she stands at 4'11" and weighs all of 91 pounds. She still competes and adds awards and accolades to her already enormous list of notable athletic accomplishments. She is the reigning world champion in the world of gymnastics. Of course, anyone who has accomplished as much as Shannon Miller has endured hardships in order to reach such a level of expertise.

It is interesting to note that wisdom passed on by Olympic athletes often comes from youngsters who have fostered a winning spirit early in their lives. To sit at the feet of a champion and gather "how to" information is a privileged honor, regardless of the champion's age. One can read between the lines of Shannon Miller's letter and get an understanding of her heart.

Mr. Andy Andrews
P.O. Box 2761
Gulf Shores, AL 36547

Dear Andy,

When I received a letter from you asking if I could share a difficult time in my life, it wasn't hard to decide what experience I wanted to share. While I've certainly had a wonderful experience as a competitive gymnast, enjoying seeing so much of the world, meeting people from different cultures and other talented athletes, and of course feeling the exhilaration of winning for my country, there have also been some tough times. Many sports fans probably remember when I injured my elbow a few months before the 1992 Olympics and had to have surgery to put a screw in it. This was a frightening time, as Olympic Trials were so close, and I had worked so many years for an opportunity to earn a place on the Team, but one of the most frustrating times of my career actually occurred **after** the Olympics.

In February of 1994, I was training hard for World Championships. I had won the All Around at the 1993 World Championships in Birmingham, England, and felt I had a great chance to make U.S. history by winning a second World All Around Title. Training was going well. My back was not bothering me nearly as much as it had in Birmingham. While I had shin splints, they had not gotten severe and I could handle the pain. I had two new front tumbling passes in my floor routine and a new move on bars, along with a new vault. I planned to try out my new skills at the American Cup Competition in Orlando in late February and felt I'd be in great shape for World Championships in Brisbane, Australia, in early April.

Suddenly, a few days before the American Cup, I pulled a stomach muscle. The pain was so severe, I could not even do a 'kip' on bars, and tumbling on floor and beam was extremely difficult. It became clear very quickly that I wouldn't be able to compete at the American Cup. This was devastating because the rules stated that I had to finish in the top six on at least one event at the American Cup to qualify for the World Championship Team. With only five weeks until World's, my coach and I hoped that if I rested the stomach muscle for about two weeks, I'd be able to begin training again and get ready for World's in the few weeks that were left. But first I would have to qualify at the American Cup.

My coach and I experimented and discovered Vault seemed to hurt the least. We decided to work Vault (only as much as necessary) and to compete that one event in an attempt to achieve at least a sixth place finish.

At the American Cup, I did the new vault, a Yurchenko Arabian, and landed it both times pretty well, in fact, I attained the highest Vault score only to discover there was confusion on the vault number flashed by my coach. Even though the judges admitted the new vault code was unclear, they decided that the wrong vault number was posted and deducted three tenths of a point from each vault. I dropped from first to ninth place - and off the World's Team! Trying to think of some way to qualify, I went to beam and began trying to warm up a beam routine, but I had not even tried a beam routine for many weeks. In the meantime, a Romanian gymnast's coach had made exactly the same mistake as my coach. However, he was informed before her second vault and she received only one deduction. After a lengthy conference, it was decided that I should not receive the deduction on my second vault. When the scores were added up, I had jumped to fourth place and on to the USA World Championship Team. One hurdle down!

Back in gym, I eased up on training for a week to let the stomach muscle heal. It started feeling better and I started training a little harder only to discover my stomach protesting. So I eased off again for two more weeks. Time was running out and I still couldn't go all out. When I got on the airplane for Australia, I still had not done a complete bar routine and had done only one full floor set (the day before we left).

We had about a week in Australia before the first competition. Workouts were rough for me, even the TV commentators noticed that my coaches and I struggled during that week. But neither my coaches, Steve and Peggy, nor I ever gave up. I didn't have to compete in this meet. I had won medals in two previous World Championships and in the Olympics. My chance of repeating as the All Around World Champion was slim even if I was in superb shape. After the qualifying session, I could have chosen to skip the All Around and concentrate on just the events for which I was most prepared, Vault and Beam. But neither Steve, Peggy or I has ever taken the easy way out.

I know that God is always with me, and I truly believe that he makes sure that we are always in the our right place. If my place was in a stadium in Brisbane, Australia, then he was there to guide me in everything I did. With confidence in my coaches to train me in the best way possible, and trust in God to look after all of us, I knew that the World Championships would be a wonderful experience regardless of the outcome. I did compete in the All Around session and won the Gold medal. While this surprised a lot of people who had watched my struggles, and perhaps even myself a little bit, my biggest achievement came on the beam during individual apparatus finals. Training on the hard mats had caused my shin splints to become extremely painful. I could hardly walk and my coaches were considering withdrawing me from the event. I insisted on competing, went up second and hit one of the best beam routines that I have ever done in competition. I was certainly very happy with those two gold medals!

In my room, I keep a card that a fan sent me. It's a quotation from Paul 'Bear' Bryant: "If you believe in yourself and have dedication and pride - and never quit, you'll be a winner. The price of victory is high - but so are the rewards."

Shannon Miller

*"You can make more friends
in two months by becoming
more interested in other
people than you can in two
years by trying to get people
interested in you."*

Dale Carnegie

TOM LANDRY

**FORMER HEAD COACH
DALLAS COWBOYS**

*...received the highest honor
awarded to a member of his
profession when he became an
inductee to the Pro Football
Hall of Fame in 1990.*

A true blooded Texan, Tom Landry was born and raised in Mission, Texas. After a successful high school football career, Tom flew thirty B-17 combat missions in World War II. Upon his return from the war, his love of football and talent for the game drew him back to the gridiron.

Tom joined the Dallas Cowboys as head coach in 1960. He soon became known as an innovator and was hailed as the best defensive coach in the business. Tom Landry revised not only several tactics of the game, but also revised the spirit of his players. During his 29 consecutive years as the head coach of "America's Team," Tom guided the Dallas Cowboys to 20 consecutive winning seasons, 18 playoff appearances, 13 division championships, 5 NFC titles and the victories in Super Bowls VI and XII. In 1990, Tom Landry was inducted into the Pro Football Hall of Fame.

Tom Landry's stature in the coaching profession remains unsurpassed. The amazing and significant thing about Tom is his ability, both from a football and personal standpoint, to change with the times. His dedication and persistence is an encouraging example of his approach to tough times.

Tom Landry
Dallas, Texas

Andy Andrews
P.O. Box 2761
Gulf Shores, AL 36547

Dear Andy:

In 1960, the NFL Expansion Committee, headed by Chicago Bears' owner George Halas, did not want to allow the new American Football League a head start in the Texas market. The Dallas franchise became the first expansion club in a long while.

The Dallas Texans were already established as an American League team. The college draft was over with at the time we received our franchise.

The NFL Owners decided to stock the new Dallas franchise with three players from each team. George Halas had already drafted Don Meredith and Don Perkins on the Bears 3rd and 5th choice. We received both players by returning Dallas' third and fifth choice the following year.

We didn't have too many talented players in 1960. Our season record was 0-11-1. Tex Schramm, our general manager, and our owner, Clint Murchison, expected to turn out a winning team within three years. It didn't happen. Our best record for five years was five wins in 1962 and 1964.

By 1964, our fans and media felt like they needed a new coach. Mr. Murchison called a press conference and gave me a ten year contract plus one year I had left on my old contract.

The following year, 1965, we had a 7-7 record and went to the now defunct runner-up bowl. In 1966 we started what would become a 20 year winning streak. In 1966 and 1967, we lost the championship which would have allowed us to play in the first Super Bowl game. The Green Bay Packers beat us both years in two great games. Both games were decided in the last two minutes -- the "Ice game," in 1967, was decided by Bart Starr's QB sneak.

The media started to label us as "the team that couldn't win the big game." I guess we started to believe it. We lost the next two years in the playoffs to the Cleveland Browns.

The following year, 1970, we played the St. Louis Cardinals on a Monday night. The Cardinals' record was 7-1 and the Cowboys were struggling with a 5-3 record. We knew we had to win to have any reasonable hope of capturing our division title and making the playoffs.

Playing on our home field, in front of millions of viewers around the nation, the Cardinals humiliated us by a score of 38-0. The following day our team met in our meeting room. Every head was looking to the floor. I tried every way to get them up, so I finally told the squad "Let's go out and play touch football." They became relaxed and we went out the next week and defeated the Washington Redskins by a score of 45-21. We won all the rest of our games and passed the Cardinals and went to our first Super Bowl.

Winston Churchill spoke to his alma mater a number of years after World War II. He was old and had trouble getting up to the podium. Then he spoke "Never give up, Never -- Never -- Never" and returned to his seat.

Sincerely,

Tom Landry

ALPHABETICAL INDEX

For booking information,
additional copies of this series,
or to see other popular items by Andy Andrews
such as comedy cassettes, motivational tapes
and a variety of t-shirts, please call for a free color brochure.

1-800-726-ANDY

24 hours a day

or you may write to:

Andy Andrews

P.O. Box 17321

Nashville, TN 37217

USA